Critical Guides to French Texts

76 Maupassant: Bel-Ami

Critical Guides to French Texts

EDITED BY ROGER LITTLE, WOLFGANG VAN EMDEN,
DAVID WILLIAMS

MAUPASSANT

Bel-Ami

Christopher Lloyd

Lecturer in French,
University of Durham

Grant & Cutler Ltd
1988

© Grant & Cutler Ltd
1988
ISBN 0 7293 0293 8

I.S.B.N. 84-599-2535-8

DEPÓSITO LEGAL: V. 2.608 - 1988

Printed in Spain by
Artes Gráficas Soler, S.A. - La Olivereta, 28 - 46018 Valencia

for

GRANT & CUTLER LTD
55-57, GREAT MARLBOROUGH STREET, LONDON W1V 2AY

Contents

Prefatory Note

A N Y O N E setting out to write a critical guide to a well-known work of literature has to steer a perilous course between the Scylla of condescending superficiality and the Charybdis of abstruse allusiveness if he does not wish to bore the specialist scholars who will consult his study and at the same time baffle the general reader. In writing this book, I have tried to eschew the rather solemn manner and difficult jargon which are found in some academic criticism, adopting instead a more colloquial and sceptical tone, in the hope that the reader may occasionally be entertained as well as informed. Though I try to show some of the weaknesses of *Bel-Ami* as a novel, and expose the equivocal nature of its creator's attitudes in some areas (particularly concerning women and social and political issues), I would not, needless to say, have written this book if I did not think *Bel-Ami* a good novel, worthy of serious study, and feel a great admiration for the consummate literary craftsmanship of Guy de Maupassant.

I have also tried on occasion to persuade the reader, particularly the reader studying literature in pursuit of an educational qualification, to think about what he or she is seeking to gain from this activity. Consequently I have made a certain number of observations which may seem provocative or irrelevant; they are not meant to be so. The essential purpose of a critical guide, of course, is to provide and promote close analysis of a literary text. Experience suggests that while many readers of *Bel-Ami* respond strongly to the characters in the novel, they pay less attention to its structure and historical background. Two out of the three main chapters of this book are therefore devoted to these latter aspects.

There are several good editions of *Bel-Ami* currently available. References to the text in this study are therefore simply followed by part and chapter numbers. Italicised figures in parentheses, followed where appropriate by volume and page numbers, refer to the bibliography at the end of this book. Place of publication of all works cited is Paris, unless otherwise stated.

Finally, I would like to thank Dr Peter Whyte and Professor Roger Little for their helpful comments during the preparation of this study.

1

Maupassant and *Bel-Ami*

A sultry summer evening in Paris in the 1880s. Humid waves of heat bounce between the pavements and buildings, carrying the stench of the sewers and basement kitchens open to the street. Into this atmosphere, with an air of seedy heroism, emerges Georges Duroy, an itchy lust in his loins and the change from five francs in his pocket. He is wearing a sixty-franc suit, a top-hat set at a raffish angle but which has seen better days; he thrusts his way through the crowd with a swagger both aggressive and self-conscious, inspecting the women, who in turn cast admiring glances at his blue eyes, curly reddish-blond hair, frizzy moustache and solid masculine figure. By the end of the chapter, he has added forty francs to his depleted finances, had his woman, and taken the first steps that, by the end of the novel, will lead him back to the Madeleine, his initial destination and the scene of his final moment of triumph.

A caddish adventurer prowling the streets of Paris in the singularly ill-named Belle Epoque, with its bad drains and sleazy tenements, its rampant prostitution and destitution, its political opportunism and repression. Duroy, the peasant turned *sous-officier* turned clerk in a railway company, struggling to hold on to his gentility, is a fitting product of this world which the opening chapter of Maupassant's second novel *Bel-Ami* evokes with dexterous economy. It thrusts us on to the street with the hero and drives the narrative forward with a rapidity that creates a pace and tone quite different from the novels often cited as models for *Bel-Ami* – the leisurely and elaborate exploration of the topography and sociology of Verrières and the 'maison Vauquer' by Stendhal in *Le Rouge et le Noir* (1830) and Balzac in *Le Père Goriot*

(1835) respectively, or the journey by steamer down the Seine with which Flaubert begins *L'Education sentimentale* (1869), symbolically suggesting the drifting passivity of his hero Frédéric Moreau and the monotonous flow of the events that surround him. Georges Duroy, as this exposition suggests, is far from being a rebel against the society of the Third Republic; he is the predator temporarily unable to satisfy his appetites. His experience in North Africa has taught him that the lives of three Arabs are worth about twenty chickens and a couple of sheep and he is perfectly willing to strangle a passer-by for his money. From the beginning, Duroy imposes himself on the reader as a strong physical and moral (or amoral) presence, whose adventures on the one hand represent the fulfilment of his appetites, the cultivation of a certain image of worldly success, and on the other allow the author to comment, usually implicitly, on the society which stimulates and upholds these appetites and such an image. Duroy's conquest, as he moves from the pavement of the rue Notre-Dame de Lorette to the steps of the Madeleine (both names evoke, appropriately enough, sexual exploitation and prostitution), is that of an urban space – the Paris of the Right Bank, the glamour of the boulevards, the Folies-Bergère, the world of journalism and finance. His final aspiration is to extend his territory by crossing the river to the Palais-Bourbon and entering the Chamber of Deputies.

Maupassant's technical facility has of course always gained him public appeal and critical scorn (Edmond de Goncourt observed sourly that a page of Maupassant could have been written by anybody). The opening scenes of *Bel-Ami* are memorable and striking – the Parisian tableaux which combine squalor and glamour in equal measure, the surprise encounters with Forestier and Rachel – yet they are never very far from the hackneyed images of the naturalist and popular novel in the second half of the nineteenth century. Maupassant's contemporary Huysmans, for instance, had already tried his hand at nocturnal street scenes and the Folies-Bergère in works like *En ménage* (1881) and *Croquis parisiens* (1880). The author himself points out to us that with his roguish charm, Duroy 'ressemblait bien au mauvais

sujet du roman populaire' (I,1). Anticipating criticism, however, does not necessarily alter its validity. Paul Ignotus
assures us that Maupassant 'rings like gold when he speaks
about cheap coin' and that 'Flaubert's style, like his philo-
sophy, was watered down by his disciple. [...] But its very
deterioration reflected an advance both in readability and in
practical wisdom' (*43* pp. 73, 110). Here, in fact, two serious
problems arise with *Bel-Ami*: a certain hollowness in its main
character, whatever his physical attractiveness, which may be
defined in either moral or psychological terms, but which in
any case makes it hard to find much gold among the base
coin; and the author's reluctance to set up the barriers to
readability which one finds, in different ways, in Stendhal,
Balzac or Flaubert, a reluctance which exposes him to accusations of superficiality and glibness, of formula-writing, or
even of 'a fundamental lack of intelligence', as Martin Tur-
nell unkindly puts it (*51*, p. 117). Maupassant's provocative
(and untruthful) boasts that he wrote only for money – 'Je
suis un industriel des lettres' he proclaimed sardonically
(quoted in *48*, p. 345) – do not help his case. The modern
reader, besides, probably has a masochistic suspicion that
writing that is not 'difficult' is somehow lacking in nutritive
value; but even if one wants to avoid paying ritual obeisance
to the demands of modern criticism by making Maupassant a
'problematic' writer, one can with a certain satisfaction discover plenty of problems in *Bel-Ami* which are worthy of the
attention of the conscientious reader.

The most obvious example is probably the autobiographical approach. A recent popular biography of Maupassant
tells us loudly that *Bel-Ami, c'est moi*! (*13*, echoing Flaubert's
apocryphal quip 'Madame Bovary, c'est moi'); Armand Lanoux had already written an excellent study of *Maupassant le
Bel-Ami,* so the reminder was unnecessary. Maupassant was
indeed fond of identifying himself with his unscrupulous
hero, with varying degrees of seriousness; he signs himself
'Bel-Ami' on a dedication of the novel; more interestingly,
as Lanoux observes,

Le cynique Maupassant ne plaisantait pas avec l'eau, élément
sacré. Or, *Bel-Ami lui-même* est l'homme qui baptise *Bel-
Ami* son premier yacht, signe de sa fortune et de sa puissance,
justement acheté avec l'argent du roman. (*48*, pp. 285-86)

But Maupassant also wanted to call one of his houses 'La
Maison Tellier', until his mother dissuaded him, without
presumably considering himself to be a brothel-keeper. To
identify a yacht with a novel is in any case not the same as
identifying oneself, with a rather self-deprecating humour,
with a fictional character – the baptism of the yacht seems to
be a grateful, if slightly derisory, tribute to the success and
financial freedom Maupassant had gained through literature.
Clearly, *Bel-Ami* is not an autobiographical novel in the
sense that there is a one-to-one correspondence between the
author and his hero and the events of their lives. On the other
hand, it is a truism to say that all authors put themselves into
their novels, in one way or another.

What is more interesting, at this preliminary stage of
investigation, is to marshal some evidence in the case of
Maupassant versus Bel-Ami: not only does our understanding
of the character depend largely on our ability to analyse the
curious blend of sympathy and repulsion which narrator and
reader are led to feel for him, but our appreciation of the
major themes of the novel also demands investigation of the
curious way Maupassant simultaneously exalts and devalues
success gained through writing and sexual conquest. In *Bel-
Ami,* Maupassant is not simply satirising an unscrupulous
group of journalists and politicians from a safe distance; their
world is his world, as most contemporary critics realised
when they took the book to be a *roman à clé.* Yet this world
is built on fraud: Duroy is a deceiver most obviously as a
writer, but writing itself seems to be little more than a lie, in
the milieu of *La Vie française,* a title which suggests the
French reader cannot escape collusion with an inauthentic
universe, for it is his universe. Duroy's sexuality is strangely
equivocal; he is someone who proves his worth by gazing at
the images which the world reflects back at him – as 'Bel-
Ami', or the fantastic millionaire in one of many mirrors –

but whose identity tends indeed to dissolve into these reflections. Perhaps, like the illusionism of fiction which Maupassant defined in an essay on the novel, all literature and the success it brings is a mirage.

At the simplest level, then, how far does Duroy bear any resemblance to Maupassant as he was in 1885? Duroy is tall, fair, and endowed with a sexual magnetism that attracts women in a way that may seem fantastic to those of us who do not possess it (some critics do in fact see the novel, for all its low realism, as verging on a sort of fantastic wish fulfilment). Maupassant himself, who contracted syphilis in about 1877 and died before he reached the age of forty-three in a lunatic asylum, after suffering increasingly over many years from a variety of probably related illnesses, was short, dark and squat, with slightly bloated features, a thick neck, and a muscular physique which in photographs gives his clothes an uncomfortably tight appearance. Professional wrestlers are said to have admired his biceps, and intimates were treated to displays of his erectile powers (Léon Bloy dubbed him the 'ithyphallic novelist'). The journalist Jules Huret met him in 1891, just before the end admittedly, and found him singularly unprepossessing. These details do perhaps have more than an anecdotal interest, in that *Bel-Ami* is at first sight at least a novel about the physical aspects of sexual attraction. Maupassant has both idealised his own experience and, more significantly, submitted it to a process of euphemistic attenuation: chronic sickness is transferred to Forestier; Duroy's erotic charms depend on his ability to display the plumage of the 'beau mâle', and not on his prowess in copulation. This particular shift of emphasis is due to more than a desire to follow the conventions of respectable Victorian literature; the novel may be titillating, but there is little or no exploration of sexual passion (excepting perhaps the case of Mme Walter).

Morally, Duroy must be one of the most reptilian characters in French literature. He plagiarises much of his journalistic material from his wife Madeleine (biographers who wonder whether Maupassant likewise exploited his secretary Clémence Brun, or other women friends, seem somewhat ingenuous, though in the manuscript of *Bel-Ami* Madeleine is first called 'Clémence': see *4*); when his mistress Mme de Marelle denounces his rapacity, he gives her a beating. Maupassant himself despised men who struck women, just as he considered men who fought duels and aspired to politics to be mostly rogues and fools. Duroy does eventually learn to write, but only in a journalistic fashion, which seems to demand a sort of coded dishonesty. Although he published some two hundred articles and three hundred stories in newspapers, and consequently had to obey the demands of such a medium, Maupassant himself in an article on the press tried to rescue 'literature' from such ephemera and place it in a more hallowed position – the true novelist must refuse all compromise, he maintained (*6,* III, p. 42). There are certain moments in *Bel-Ami* when Maupassant seems deliberately to stress the yawning gap between his own creative vitality and the paltry efforts of Duroy. Contemplating the glory of a Mediterranean sunset, Duroy is unable to find an expression more capable of evoking his admiration than 'c'est épatant, ça!' (I, 8); the author, on the other hand, has created the sensuous beauty of this scene in a page of bravura description. Similarly, Duroy's inability to compose the articles requested by Walter in an earlier passage is teasingly contrasted with the narrator's deft evocation of the very memories of North Africa which defy Duroy's attempts to trap them on paper (I, 3).

To identify Duroy with Maupassant, then, we have to accept an odd combination: the character is physically idealised, and yet morally debased, compared with his creator. Critics have of course found many other models for Duroy. Three who are most frequently cited perhaps shed some light on the ambivalence with which Duroy is seen. They are the journalists René Maizeroy and the Baron de Vaux, and Maupassant's brother Hervé. Maupassant was close enough to the first two to write sympathetic prefaces to their books; but by all accounts both seem to have been pretty dubious characters, the first using his lady-friends to help write his articles, and the 'Baron', a former *sous-officier* and 'faux gentilhomme', having a sideline in blackmail (see *46,* pp. 289 ff.). For Hervé, again a former N.C.O., Maupassant is also said to have felt 'une sorte d'horreur sympathique' (*53,* p. 11). To play the game of matching fictional characters and real people was doubtless great fun for contemporary readers who were in the know. A century later, however, it is both difficult and not very relevant – the novel, in this sense, is one of lost allusions, if not of lost illusions. In any case, Georges Duroy (the only true 'type' created by the naturalist novel, according to Thibaudet, *58,* p. 227) is now far more famous than his models, just as Robert de Montesquiou is remembered largely as the model for Huysmans' des Esseintes and Proust's Charlus.

Before concluding this discussion of the autobiographical aspects of *Bel-Ami,* it is worth looking at an article on this subject by Maupassant himself which is not often cited. Talking in June 1883 about novels clearly based on actual events and people, Maupassant argues that the function of the novelist is to universalise, to achieve a neutral objectivity:

> Le romancier n'est pas un moraliste: il n'a pas mission pour corriger ou modifier les mœurs. Son rôle se borne à observer et à décrire, suivant son tempérament, selon les limites de son talent. Viser quelqu'un, c'est faire un acte déshonnête, comme artiste d'abord, comme homme ensuite. Mais prendre dans chaque existence les anecdotes et les observations qui nous intéressent, et s'en servir dans le roman en ne laissant point deviner les acteurs véritables, en démarquant, pour ainsi dire, le fait arrivé, c'est faire acte d'artiste consciencieux; et personne ne peut se blesser de ce procédé. (*6,* II, p. 216)

This article is entitled 'Les Masques', because the novelist's fiction is a mask, a stylised representation of reality, which both conceals historical and biographical fact, yet also offers occasional titillating glimpses of it. Maupassant, however, at the same time recognises that the mask creates a moral ambiguity; the writer constantly feels the urge to rip apart the mask of conventional decorum and morality to expose the dishonesty and self-deception which he considers to be the governing forces of human relations, casting himself as a latter-day La Rochefoucauld:

Toute action humaine est une manifestation d'égoïsme dégui-
sée. Le mérite de l'action ne vient que du déguisement. [...]
Certains hommes croient au déguisement que la morale met
sur nos actes: ce sont les honnêtes gens. ("Le Fond du cœur",
6, III, p. 28)

In this sense, Bel-Ami is indeed everybody's fine friend:
'Bel-Ami, c'est vous!' one might say, as with an ingenuous
charm he learns the social and cultural codes which turn
ruthlessness into civilised honesty. Villainy is the other side
of the mask of the perfect 'honnête homme'. Maupassant's
ultimate aim, then, in *Bel-Ami* is to encompass specific
historical and biographical fact and fictional universality, or,
to put it less flatly, to move with a rather cruel playfulness (if
one considers that Duroy, apart from his pretty face, is a sort
of stunted caricature of some of Maupassant's own aspirations and achievements) from teasing allusions to an exemplary portrait of the ruthless egotism which the individual
needs to display to survive and succeed in human society. Far
from denouncing the corruption of groups or the self-centred
and hypocritical cruelty of the *arriviste,* Maupassant may
well see them as the products of a dynamic necessity which
sweeps aside the sentimental morality of the average reader.
The reader, on the other hand, may be inclined to think that
Maupassant's attempts to give his vitalistic pessimism a
Schopenhauerian grandeur tend to collapse into a rather
commonplace nastiness.

For one commentator, in fact, Bel-Ami and his creator
enjoy an 'accord voluptueux' (5, p. 12). At the end of the
novel, Duroy, or Du Roy, undergoes his final apotheosis
before a worshipping crowd in the Madeleine: he is the
secular King of Kings, messiah of mediocrity. As the sacra-
ment is performed, we are told, 'l'Homme-Dieu [...] descen-
dait sur la terre pour consacrer le triomphe du baron Georges
Du Roy' (II, 10). We have already seen Mme Walter praying
before a picture of Christ which resembles Duroy (II, 7) –
Christ resembling Duroy, and not Duroy Christ. Not only is
Maupassant defining a new naturalist ethic, but in this
conclusion he seems to be striving to raise the adventure of
his *arriviste* to the level of a myth which supplants the old

myth of Christianity. Even if one remains sceptical about the validity of this ambition (the novel contains too many uncertainties to carry off such aspirations), at least it helps to differentiate *Bel-Ami* from its predecessors as the story of an *arriviste*. Once again, there are doubtless innumerable potential sources or points of comparison, from Marivaux's *Le Paysan parvenu* in 1734-35 to John Braine's *Room at the Top* in 1957 (like Maupassant, Braine has a strong feeling for the material texture and social status of luxury goods, and objects usually come with a price-tag attached). But the Balzac of *Le Père Goriot* and *Illusions perdues* (1837-43) (see *24*), and the Stendhal of *Le Rouge et le Noir* are the points of reference most frequently cited. One could also cite Stendhal's *Lucien Leuwen* (1834-35) or Flaubert's *L'Education sentimentale.*

In terms of imaginative power or depth of understanding, Stendhal, Balzac and Flaubert make Maupassant look like a pygmy as a novelist. Nevertheless, such comparisons are most useful if, as already suggested, they allow us to see how Maupassant steps out of the shadow of his predecessors and creates a work that is distinctive and different, even if it is not a masterpiece. Some critics tend, on the contrary, to underplay Maupassant's originality in *Bel-Ami*. Walter, of course, is compared to a character in Balzac in the text itself (I, 4), but André Vial's observation that his henchman Forestier 'joue auprès de Duroy le rôle de Vautrin auprès de Rastignac' (*60*, p. 298), still seems rather sweeping. The moribund and mediocre Forestier, himself largely the creation of his wife Madeleine, is hardly a match for the protean vigour of Vautrin, alias Jacques Collin, alias 'Trompe-la-Mort'. It might be interesting, on the other hand, to consider the equivocal sexual aspects of Vautrin's relations with Rastignac and the strange triangle of Forestier, Madeleine and Duroy. Vial makes a more telling point when he argues that both Maupassant and Balzac achieve a symbiosis between character and a historical moment, whereas Flaubert in *L'Education sentimentale* merely shows a parallelism between private individuals and public events.

Again, Gérard Delaisement suggests an analogy between Duroy and Julien Sorel ('la différence n'est que de degré:

seuls comptent les résultats', *31,* p. 46) which is highly
misleading: the conclusion of *Bel-Ami* is the reverse of that of
Le Rouge et le Noir, since Julien explicitly rejects the moral
and social compromises on which Duroy thrives. Both are
egotistical upstarts, perhaps, but Julien moves in an aura of
glowing heroic energy for which Duroy's curly moustache is
hardly a match. He may be unscrupulous and ridiculous on
occasions, but he is raised far above the base mediocrity and
cynical opportunism which condition the characters of *Bel-
Ami.* It is in this last sense that one might relate *Bel-Ami* to
L'Education sentimentale, where the Balzacian adventure has
decayed into a sour recognition that mediocrity, stupidity and
self-deception are the governing forces in a world which is
betrayed by and betrays both dreamers and men of action.
But Duroy is not driven to sum up his sentimental adventures
in the derisory formula of Frédéric Moreau and Deslauriers,
'C'est là ce que nous avons eu de meilleur', as they finally
decide that an abortive visit to a brothel in their youth was
the high point of their emotional experience. Unlike Flaubert, who observed that there was no need to cross the
threshold of the kitchen of life since you knew the stench
inside would make you vomit, Maupassant did not feel the
need to turn anti-climaxes into climaxes.

Critics are, however, divided in their interpretation of the
key themes and prevailing tone of *Bel-Ami.* Duroy's sexual
rapacity may seem to place him a long way from the eager
juvenile inexperience of Julien Sorel, who bursts into tears in
Mme de Rênal's bedroom, or from the unconsummated
passion of Frédéric Moreau for Mme Arnoux. Yet, thinking
perhaps of the sinister mechanical copulatory exploits for
which Maupassant was famous (they are immortalised in his
gruesome obscene farce, *A la feuille de rose...*), Jean-Louis
Bory sees in *Bel-Ami* a spiralling cycle of predatory desire,
where climax is forever forestalled:

> Tout convoiter sans jouir de rien, ce n'est pas seulement la
> dynamique de l'ambitieux – Maupassant l'est, ambition d'une
> autre qualité mais de la même famille que l'arrivisme de
> Duroy –; c'est l'élan du pirate, de l'écumeur d'alcôves (cette

superbe image est de Paul Morand), exerçant sur la femme un droit d'épave.   (2, p. 21)

Behind the frenzied and never fulfilled *appétit de jouissance* of Duroy and his society lurks 'l'angoisse du néant' (2, p. 25), undercutting all action and achievement. At the same time, Bory argues that we cannot ignore contemporary reactions to the novel, which saw it as a virulent piece of social comment: '*Bel-Ami* est un roman politique, une satire de la démocratie capitaliste' (2, p. 17). Jacques Laurent, however, believes that 'si ce roman n'est qu'à peine politique, il est sensuel d'un bout à l'autre' (5, p. 12); Philippe Bonnefis even finds it displays a 'vivacité joyeuse' (5, p. 381).

Maupassant himself rarely seems to have felt the need to analyse his own work in his correspondence, unlike his master Flaubert. His letters generally reveal a hard-headed preoccupation with money matters, while his newspaper articles again seldom reveal much about his deeper personal feelings about his art. He began writing *Bel-Ami* in the summer of 1884. His valet François Tassart says he finished it on 26 October 1884, which seems extraordinarily rapid progress; the best edition of his correspondence *(11)* gives a completion date of 21 February 1885, which seems preferable, since the novel was serialised in the Parisian daily *Gil Blas* from 6 April to 30 May 1885 and published as a book by Havard in May 1885, two months after the other great novel of 1885, Zola's *Germinal* (also serialised in *Gil Blas*). It was in *Gil Blas* too that Maupassant published his only substantial commentary on *Bel-Ami*, 'Aux critiques de *Bel-Ami*', on 7 June 1885. Unfortunately, this article is largely an exercise in special pleading, aimed at placating those irate colleagues who felt the author had fouled the nest of journalism with Rabelaisian gusto. Maupassant's attitude towards the press will be considered in Chapter 4; suffice it to say here that he does not shed much light on the critical problems already touched upon, since his main aim seems to be to cover his tracks, to take up his mask in rather coy fashion.

'Pourquoi Maupassant a-t-il l'air de trouver si naturelle la bassesse de son triste héros?' asked A. Siegfried in 1954 (quoted in *I,* p. 404). A less hostile critic expresses the ambivalence of our attitude to Duroy more fully:

> Quand il s'avisera [...] de créer un type, son Bel-Ami, il en fera sans doute un être assez vil selon nos préjugés et nos conventions, mais il saura nous le rendre sympathique, malgré tout, et le succès de son héros, succès scandaleux, oui, je le veux bien, nous trouvera tout de même pleins d'indulgence, et peut-être de complaisance secrète ... (Georges Rency, quoted in *I,* p. 403)

More detailed examination of scenes in the text itself is needed to pursue this discussion of Maupassant's most memorable male hero. The next chapter is consequently devoted to an exploration of this character and those who surround him. The novel itself is Maupassant's most ambitious and longest work of fiction, written at the height of his creative powers (in 1884 and 1885, apart from *Bel-Ami,* he published six books of stories, not to mention forty or more newspaper articles and the travel book *Au soleil).* Its contribution to the development of French fiction and Maupassant's reputation is a point best left to the conclusion of this study. More important perhaps is the charge sometimes made against Maupassant that as a novelist he is somewhat short-winded – hence the contention that *Pierre et Jean* (1888) is by far his best novel, since it is nearest to the *nouvelle* in form (see e.g. *55,* p. 106). Such questions will be examined in the chapter on 'structures'. It is perhaps worth stressing that the nineteenth-century realist text has a supreme confidence in its own transparency: it does create a world, a world which strives to correspond closely to sociological and historical fact, a world peopled by characters we are meant to take as real. This may be a game of illusion, as Maupassant himself pointed out in an essay on the novel which prefaced *Pierre et Jean,* but it is a game we have to play on its own terms. This is not to deny that any novel is ultimately a literary construct, a symphony of words, but merely an attempt to justify the tripartite approach taken in the rest of this study – an approach through people, form, and history.

2

Characters

Ambiguity in everyday conversation or in the questions on an examination paper is liable to cause embarrassment or even panic. In literature, however, multiplicity of meaning is generally held to be a virtue, and the cleverest commentator is the one who can find the largest number of answers to the largest number of questions. To tolerate the characters of *Bel-Ami*, one needs perhaps to hold on to some notion of ambivalence. Maupassant's heroes are rarely complicated, either emotionally or intellectually; as Pol Neveux observed, in a sensitive essay published fifteen years after Maupassant's death (*10, Boule de suif*), the trenchant observation of the characters' exchanges in the stagecoach in 'Boule de suif' is infinitely more effective than the interminable analysis of the vapid sophisticates of *Fort comme la mort* and *Notre cœur*. The reader who expects to find in Maupassant the extraordinary richness or depth of feeling which Tolstoy or George Eliot create for their characters in *Anna Karenina* (1873-77) or *Middlemarch* (1871-72) is likely to be disappointed. Brunetière, in his contemporaneous study of *Le Roman naturaliste* (1883), in fact places these two authors far higher than novelists like Flaubert and Zola in the scale of achievement of realist writing: from Flaubert onwards, he complains, French realists have become obsessed with the baser aspects of human nature, and the sordid and mediocre milieu which they present debases the value of their own writing.

Such a rebuke, however moralistically old-fashioned, could no doubt be addressed to the characters of *Bel-Ami*. Whereas Julien Sorel in *Le Rouge et le Noir* and Dorothea Brooke in *Middlemarch* are clearly endowed with admirable and exceptional qualities, even if the first gives way to a criminal frenzy in shooting Mme de Rênal, and the second displays a stubborn schoolgirlish immaturity in marrying Mr Casaubon, what is most striking about Georges Duroy is surely his complete ordinariness and lack of talent. Even his sexual magnetism may fail to appeal: it works more as a mysterious force of nature (attracting women as excrement attracts flies) than as a positive virtue. Duroy is unexceptional either as a hero or a villain, although he is seen as both in the book, perhaps because, like Flaubert, and unlike Baudelaire or Huysmans, Maupassant has no real belief in good or evil, or some sort of individual transcendence. But what is also striking about Duroy is the curiously memorable nature of his adventures. Perhaps the central area of ambivalence in the book is the strong sense of charm it exerts while focusing almost continually on a protagonist who, if considered dispassionately, seems somewhat repellent. This problem suggests how apparently 'moral' issues can blend into questions of perspective and construction. Far from being a random string of episodes, *Bel-Ami* is skilfully and deliberately patterned: characters, themes, and episodes all have what one might call symphonic functions. For the moment, however, I prefer to talk about the characters in the novel as if they were real people, before looking at the economy of the novel from inside and outside in the following chapters. Since the realist text invites us to enter a world of characters and to explore their thoughts, feelings, and actions, it seems perverse to refuse to do so.

To define the charm of *Bel-Ami* and its main character is not entirely easy. In fact, it is untrue to say that Duroy is simply an ordinary man gifted with unusual physical beauty. Marcel Aymé wrote a comic novel, *La Belle Image* (1941), about a character who suddenly acquired startling physical attractiveness but who proved incapable of using this gift to do anything other than seduce his own wife, since he was completely lacking in the spirit of adventure needed to exploit his metamorphosis. Duroy, on the contrary, is shown from the beginning to possess a predatory ruthlessness, a chameleon-like adaptability, and a sense of timing which allow him to exploit any situation which promises sexual, social and financial fulfilment to his advantage, even when his self-assurance is near breaking point. Sex, success and money are of course invariably interlinked; all reflect the gratification of desire and appetite and allow a progressively enhanced set of redefinitions of the self. Appearances too are vital: what Duroy seems to be is far more important than what he really is, although the ever widening gap between the two is psychologically and morally disturbing.

From the first chapter, the deceitfulness which seems to be an integral part of his character (Edmond de Goncourt included in his long list of complaints about Maupassant the fact that he was a compulsive liar) emerges as an important factor in his success. Having gained access for the first time to the glamorous but sleazy world of the Folies-Bergère, he makes his first conquest in the shape of the prostitute later named as Rachel. The five women whom Duroy seduces in the course of the novel (Rachel, Mme de Marelle, Madeleine, Mme Walter, Suzanne Walter) all of course are meant to represent ever higher rungs on the social ladder, a conspectus of women which at first sight seems both unpleasant and conventional, since the ultimate prize is the silly doll-like virgin Suzanne, a sexual and financial commodity who in reality is probably more of an object than a common prostitute is. It is far from clear whether Maupassant actually wants the reader to make this sort of distanced judgement. The five women also reflect in a more interesting way different types of female sexuality, from the blatantly provocative Rachel to the ingenuous Suzanne. Maupassant, of course, is suggestive rather than explicit in these matters, but the initial description of Rachel, with her thrusting bosom and 'ses lèvres peintes, rouges comme une plaie' (I, 1), is both caricatural (the prostitute's exaggerated make-up parodies sexual display signals in the interests of commerce) and yet also conveys more arousingly obscene possibilities (Maupassant would on occasion sign off letters to an intimate ladyfriend 'je te baise sur toutes tes lèvres', see *11*). At the first meeting with Rachel, Duroy is tongue-tied and lies about how much money he has, as he does even more blatantly on their second meeting (I, 4). This meanness culminates in the comic confrontation in Chapter 5 between Rachel and Mme de Marelle, when Duroy receives a humiliating dressing-down from Rachel after pretending to ignore her at the Folies-Bergère. While the prostitute appears generous and forthright in this scene, Duroy reveals a fundamental weakness and dishonesty, as well as a singular ineptitude in awkward situations. This dishonesty in personal relations increases to a monumental degree as the book progresses.

Rachel caustically dismisses Duroy as a 'dos vert' (I, 6), that is, a *maquereau,* a pimp, in a telling insult, for it is at this point that having lyingly told Mme de Marelle he has spent all his money supporting his decrepit old father he begins taking money off her. Duroy of course derives much more spectacular financial benefits from his relations with Madeleine and Mme Walter and Suzanne; in fact the financial benefits increase more or less in proportion as genuine desire or emotion decrease in these exchanges, or rather, desire is increasingly channelled into the urge for social and financial profit. Thus Duroy avoids sleeping with Suzanne during their elopement, perhaps because her virginity is too great a prize to be lightly sacrificed; he is enraged when Mme de Marelle accuses him of having deflowered her, for 'cette petite fille qui allait devenir sa femme' (II, 10) barely has a sexual identity (with rather chilling naivety, she considers their six-day platonic idyll by the Seine to typify marriage with Duroy). It is also important to note that by preserving the innocence of his child-wife, Duroy is able to maintain the façade of honourable behaviour which seems to be a vital part of his self-respect. (The shock of sexual initiation for innocent brides in the Victorian era should not be forgotten: the story 'Enragée?' depicts such a situation with cruel humour.)

André Vial has drawn attention to the conflict between 'la conscience du personnage et son pouvoir économique' in *Bel-Ami* (quoted in *1,* p. 103, n. 1), studying, for example, Duroy's reactions to Vaudrec's legacy to Madeleine (*60,*

p. 387). But one wonders whether there is any question of conscience at all in such scenes: Duroy is singularly free from any sense of remorse or agony, except when his own self-preservation is at stake – before the duel, or during Forestier's death, for instance. What one really sees is a hypocritical scrupulousness, as Duroy struggles to manipulate the conventions of the social game convincingly. He may feel 'humiliation' at taking Mme de Marelle's money (I, 5), but still continues to spend it and is even able to exploit the situation in such a way that *she* is forced to apologise for letting him use her money. When, a chapter later, he meets her husband, he feels 'une joie de voleur qui a réussi' (I, 6). Vial's interpretation of the way in which Duroy appropriates half of Vaudrec's legacy again seems somewhat indulgent. Duroy's interrogation of Madeleine is particularly base (if Vaudrec left her a million, she must have been his mistress, and this inference – which is never proved true, incidentally – is unacceptable to the double standards of a male-oriented society). It is his preoccupation with conventions which he himself breaks with gay abandon that is both mean and petty, especially as greed appears to be the essential motive behind his debate. Madeleine's refusal to promote this supposed debate with conscience ('Moi, je n'ai qu'à me taire. C'est à toi de réfléchir', II, 6) surely implies a contemptuous awareness of Duroy's character which the reader is invited to share. In a final moment of petty meanness, he suggests beating down Vaudrec's nephew's demand for a share of the loot by half – a suggestion which she again curtly rejects.

The richer Duroy becomes, the cheaper he seems, in fact ('à force de voler bas, il monte haut', as Jean-Louis Bory puts it, *2,* p. 11). For another commentator, he is 'ce caractère cruellement mou' (*12,* p. 238). In the novel itself, he already receives a pretty bad press: 'Vous êtes l'être le plus vil que je connaisse' declares the spurned Mme Walter in melodramatic fashion (II, 10). 'Quel gredin tu es!' says Mme de Marelle, adding that he is a 'crapule' (II, 10), while earlier he was a 'cochon' (I, 5). 'Ah! le gredin, comme il nous a joués' muses Walter, himself a model of crooked double-dealing, adding 'C'est un homme d'avenir. Il sera député et ministre' (II, 9).

Maupassant himself, in the article 'Aux critique de *Bel-Ami*', observes that

> Je montre dès les premières lignes qu'on a devant soi une graine de gredin, qui va pousser dans le terrain où elle tombera. Ce terrain est un journal. (6, III, p. 165)

Such pejorative comments are of course double-edged: Mme de Marelle's anger contains a strong element of erotic admiration ('Elle murmura, frémissante: –Oh! comme tu es roué et dangereux, toi!', II, 10), and their quarrels, though violent, take on a ritualistic quality since reconciliation invariably follows. Walter's comment is the compliment one rogue pays to another, while Maupassant's assessment uses a naturalist's image which significantly stresses the role of environment and acclimatisation – he too sees Duroy as a healthy plant, and plants have no need of scruples and moral dilemmas. To point out that bourgeois morality is not sanctioned by any absolute, but is simply an ideological construct used to maintain the power of the ruling order, is hardly more than a truism ('Quels gredins que les honnêtes gens!' is the conclusion drawn at the end of Zola's *Le Ventre de Paris,* 1873). One could cite novels whose heroes strive to create their own ethic – usually in a self-destructive fashion – from the wreckage of a society which has outlived its values, such as Laclos's *Les Liaisons dangereuses* (1782), or among Maupassant's contemporaries, Huysmans' *A rebours* (1884) or Darien's *Le Voleur* (1897). Clearly Duroy too is a sort of thief, but unlike the anarchic, intensely individualistic heroes of these three texts, he is a hero who seems desperately eager to parade his honesty, however spurious it may be, and who seems hidebound by the very conventions whose hollowness is exposed by the novel.

Thus when Mme de Marelle confronts him in their final quarrel with the list of his villainies, he replies with an ingenuousness that is perhaps almost genuine: 'J'avais une femme qui me trompait. Je l'ai surprise; j'ai obtenu le divorce et j'en épouse une autre. Quoi de plus simple?' (II, 10). Duroy is not prepared to admit that he is a 'crapule' (he has after all betrayed his pact with Madeleine by exposing her adultery to the police while practising adultery himself, he has accepted a decoration from her lover, and then ruined his career, he has deceived Mme Walter and hoodwinked her daughter). He is quite content to live by appearances and ignore the unpleasant realities they conceal. In fact, his success consists precisely in turning appearance into reality; the image he presents to the world becomes the real man, as the name 'Bel-Ami' suggests. Just as he becomes a baron by inventing a title and country estate for himself, so too we can predict with Walter that he will become a successful politician.

Jean Prévost has argued in *La Création chez Stendhal* that when a novel is presented almost exclusively from the viewpoint of a single character, it is hard for the reader to deny this character his sympathy. In other words, we could condemn Duroy in a moral, objective sense while simultaneously obtaining a vicarious thrill from the account of his ambitions and adventures (just as he continually wins over Mme de Marelle even when she realises the depths of his baseness). Like Flaubert, Maupassant rarely if ever offers us an explicit moral judgement on his hero in the text. Flaubert, however, still expects us to arrive at judgements of his characters, and uses a variety of techniques to invite such judgements. The reader is held at a distance from characters by devices such as shifts in perspective, juxtaposition of contradictory elements, phrases that on investigation cannot be taken at face value. Despite a superficial similarity between the narrative manner of Flaubert and Maupassant, however, it is far from clear whether Maupassant expects the reader to fill in the unspoken areas of suggestion that surround details which may at first sight seem insignificant, as he is obliged to do in reading Flaubert.

'Ruiné, dépouillé, perdu!' The reader soon realises that these adjectives which begin a chapter of *L'Education sentimentale* are not an objective evaluation of Frédéric Moreau's financial situation, but the character's melodramatically self-pitying and exaggerated reaction to a setback. Similarly, when we hear Emma Bovary asking once again how she could have married the doltish Charles, 'elle qui était si intelligente', the very situation in which she asks the question makes us doubt her intelligence. It is hard to find examples in *Bel-Ami* where the reader is expected to distance himself in this way from the character and discover an implicit critical commentary on the character's behaviour. Maupassant took over Flaubert's penchant for the burlesque (Charles Bovary is obliged to conjugate 'ridiculus sum' in the first chapter of *Madame Bovary*) in certain early stories like 'Les Dimanches d'un bourgeois de Paris', but in his novels he rarely creates the ironical gap between character and narrator which is the hallmark of Flaubert's fiction. The confrontation between Duroy, Rachel and Mme de Marelle at the Folies-Bergère (recalling a similar confrontation in *L'Education sentimentale* between Frédéric, Rosanette and Mme Arnoux, where the hero looks equally pathetic) comes early in the novel, and is an unusual example of comedy at Duroy's expense. 'Georges Duroy eut le réveil triste, le lendemain' (I, 6), we are told, and this humiliation is followed by embarrassing meetings with Forestier and Rachel: in other words, the reader is soon invited to feel a certain pity for Duroy, and there is no suggestion that he has got his just deserts.

It is interesting to compare the duel scene in *Bel-Ami* with the treatment of duels in other nineteenth-century novels. In Balzac's *La Peau de chagrin* (1831) the hero Raphael despatches an adversary in a duel, despite the latter's superior skill; there is an element of drama in the combat, although the outcome is pre-ordained by the magic skin which liberates Raphael from the day-to-day concerns of the real world while imprisoning him in a superior fatality. At the end of Vallès's *Le Bachelier* (1881), Jacques Vingtras inflicts a serious wound on his closest friend in a duel which they are driven to fight in a mood of self-destructive personal and political frustration. Clearly, the duel as episode in an allegorical treatment of human destiny, or in the education of a revolutionary, may seem remote from *Bel-Ami*. Duroy's nocturnal vigil of fear, and the trivial events which oblige him to engage in ritualistic combat if he is to uphold his journalistic honour, may seem closer to the grotesque duel in *L'Education sentimentale* between Frédéric and the effete aristocrat Cisy, where both participants are as terrified as the rabbits which flee at their approach. Whereas both Vallès and Balzac endow their duels with a positive function, as part of a wider necessity, Flaubert deflates the whole notion of manly action and adventure: his absurd characters can never be more than ridiculous puppets. But while Duroy is paralysed with terror (the hero of the story 'Un lâche', which overlaps closely with this episode, blows his brains out rather than face his adversary), and simultaneously realises the absurdity of combat between total strangers, the duel in *Bel-Ami* nevertheless has a vital positive function. Duroy is driven to risk his life for appearances, and once again appearance becomes reality as, the duel marking a further degree in his initiation into journalism and worldly success, his fanciful account to Mme de Marelle of his valour becomes, after the event, both the public and private version of the truth and his cowardice is forgotten.

The difference between Flaubert and Maupassant, of course, is that Flaubert's modern heroes are invariably failures, whether of a tragic or comic variety, whereas *Bel-Ami* is about success, a success in which the author has a strong personal involvement, even if he suspects that success is merely a sham. In any case, shamming carried out with sufficient conviction is perhaps a form of success. Although Duroy's self-assurance is relatively fragile, as his nervous reaction to an unexpected appearance by Mme de Marelle after the first quarrel shows (I, 6), and his varying emotional states are described at length throughout the book, he never doubts the value of the goals which he aims for, or counts the cost of the sacrifices of basic human decency which they entail. If, as has been suggested, Duroy exerts an ambivalent seductive charm over the reader as well as the women in the book, this charm has an element of snake-like fascination – we may despise Duroy, while being overwhelmed by his impudent villainy. Maupassant's own narrative position, moreover, suggests an ambiguous moral neutrality: we do not find him condemning Duroy, or showing us how, like an Emma Bovary, he totally misjudges both his own talents and the world in which he moves. On the contrary, Duroy is at one with his world and achieves his ambitions. We have the impression, however, that Maupassant cannot make his mind up whether such achievements are valid or futile: Part I of the novel ends with the death of Forestier and passages of gloomy metaphysics that suggest that all life hastens to a hole in the ground. Yet it is from this point that Duroy's success takes off as he becomes 'Monsieur Forestier' in turn, and Part II ends with the quasi-religious triumph in the Madeleine. It is not surprising, then, that Douglas Parmée concludes that a 'dichotomy of strength and weakness, success and failure, splendour and squalor, runs as a double thread throughout the novel' (*3*, p. 5).

A further dichotomy, to recapitulate this discussion of narrative perspectives, is that between appearance and reality, *paraître* and *être*. Are we to conclude that Duroy is a totally inauthentic being, or rather that, just as conventional morality is overtaken by the law of the jungle, if one lives a lie with enough conviction one can assert a new version of the truth? Parmée again remarks that Duroy 'is shown throughout as someone who is there mainly to be *looked at* and, having been looked at, revealed inwardly and outwardly' (*3*, p. 13). The nature of the images of Duroy which are presented in the book – most notably in recurring mirrors – will be considered in the following chapter. Here, a final point worth noting is that even when Duroy is not on stage, in two brief scenes in the last two chapters, he is still the centre of attention: we see the despairing Mme Walter hallucinating in the hothouse in front of the portrait of Christ-Duroy – Christ blessing Duroy while he possesses Suzanne (II, 9) – and see the crowd gathering in the Madeleine while his colleagues sardonically enumerate the stages of his triumph (II, 10). At the end of *Madame Bovary*, we observe the degraded Emma pathetically trying to seduce the tax collector Binet in order to pay her debts from the perspective of two women watching her with malevolent curiosity through an attic window ('On devrait fouetter ces femmes-là', they conclude). These passages in *Bel-Ami*, on the contrary, seem to stand back from Duroy only to assert the sureness of his success with a near-blasphemous glee.

If one looks in more detail at Duroy's relationships with women in the novel – the apparent secret of his success – one finds again interesting areas of ambivalence, both in the presentation of Duroy as seducer and in the attitude towards women and sex which the novel conveys. The nickname 'Bel-Ami' is itself ambiguous. He is baptised one quarter of the way through the book by Mme de Marelle's pre-pubescent daughter Laurine ('C'est un bon petit nom d'amitié pour vous, ça', I, 5), whose innocent infatuation with Duroy turns sour when he marries Madeleine Forestier. She then calls him 'Monsieur Forestier' (II, 3), refusing, unlike the adults in the book, to accept his chameleon-like changes of identity. This rejection reflects a loss of innocence: Laurine (the only character to remain uncontaminated in the book) sees quite well in her childish jealousy that Duroy is using his sexual charm, not for love and friendship, but to buy his way to success. Marie-Claire Bancquart (*4*) notes that while the term 'bel ami' is used in courtly literature before the sixteenth century, in modern French it usually survives only in the feminine 'belle amie'; Laurine has translated the feminine to the masculine, implicitly recognising the feminine elements in Georges Duroy's sexual identity. As the novel progresses, other characters take up this nickname, with its simultaneous connotations of virility and prettiness, admiration and mockery. When Madeleine first calls him 'Bel-Ami', 'Il eut la sensation d'un soufflet reçu' (I, 6). But when Mme Walter uses the name (II, 3), the effect is one of coy provocation; a chapter later Walter himself is addressing Duroy by this sobriquet. Whereas Duroy recognises the nickname 'Forestier' to be an insulting reference to his strange *ménage* with Madeleine, where the ghost of the real Forestier, not to mention Vaudrec and Laroche-Mathieu, is an equivocal presence, he seems to accept that as 'Bel-Ami' he is playing the role he will be remembered for. By the last chapter he has become 'Notre Bel-Ami', achieving, as it were, universal recognition (II, 10).

The name 'Bel-Ami' thus contains a truth about Duroy which holds together positive and negative. He attracts and repels, his friendship is only skin deep, but we can never penetrate beneath the skin anyway, in Maupassant's view, and this marks him as a new type of *arriviste*. His ever-expanding real name, on the other hand (he grows from plain Georges Duroy to the baron Georges Du Roy de Cantel), may seem merely to express social pretence and chicanery. He embroiders on his plebeian birth, travelling in the opposite direction but with the same intention as a British Labour politician whose incredibly shrinking name is meant to conceal his aristocratic origins. Yet Maupassant himself held on to his own *particule* with a certain pride, and it is Madeleine Forestier, an astute player of the social and sexual game, who first asks Duroy to 'vous anoblir un peu' (II, 1), and admires him for becoming a baron (II, 6). There is more than snobbery here: though Maupassant was fond of quoting Flaubert's dictum that 'Les honneurs déshonorent' and 'Le titre dégrade' (*6,* I, p. 65), and Duroy himself flings his Legion of Honour into the fire (he starts wearing it again later), the point is that Duroy does not wait in servile fashion to be decorated for services he has not performed (like the ludicrous hero of 'Décoré!'), but aggressively ennobles himself: as his very name suggests (he was originally called 'Leroy', see *4*), the regal *arriviste* does not need others to help him promote a glittering image of nobility and potency, even if their *acknowledgement* of his success is vital. Duroy is well aware besides that the decoration which Laroche-Mathieu gives him acknowledges only his services as dupe and cuckold: far from showing base ingratitude, his bettering of the Minister consequently seems a fitting piece of revenge, a further twist in the spiral of villainy.

But is Bel-Ami as potent a hero as he appears? Parmée's reference to Duroy's 'roving penis' (*3,* p. 20) seems rather to strike a false note, given the lack of explicit reference to this organ in the text. Philippe Bonnefis, on the other hand, sees this part of Duroy's anatomy more as a gigantic crowbar ('Son sexe soulève les montagnes'), or even as a 'baguette magique' achieving miracles of wealth and favour (*5,* p. 386). Maupassant wrote explicitly about sexual acts in pornographic poems like 'Soixante-neuf' and 'La Femme à barbe', and mingles eroticism with a problematic view of sexuality in stories like 'Les Sœurs Rondoli' or 'L'Inconnue' (desire runs up against fear of venereal disease or a predatory, castrating female). His restraint in *Bel-Ami* thus seems to be deliberate: sex is a means to power, and moments of sexual pleasure are passed over discreetly in brief sentences that are hardly likely to titillate or offend the most prurient reader. One can, of course, find sexual symbols in the text which may be as revealing as more direct comments. (The reader who launches into this sort of investigation should avoid the over-interpretative zeal amusingly parodied in David Lodge's novel *Changing Places,* where an American professor exposes the erotic sub-text in Jane Austen to a bemused audience. Even Freud feels obliged to apologise for constantly reading fear of blinding as an equivalent to fear of castration in his famous essay on E.T.A. Hoffmann's story 'Der Sandmann'.)

In *Bel-Ami,* the two most striking recurrent examples of what might be seen as sexual symbolism are Duroy's moustache and (less commonly noticed by critics) the game of *bilboquet* which is all the rage at the offices of *La Vie française.* Both relate to the depiction of Duroy's potently seductive charm, and are perhaps best described as emblematic devices. Maupassant seems to have had a great faith in the erotic attraction of moustaches, perhaps after setting fire to his beard in October 1875 and contenting himself thereafter with a bushy moustache, which on photographs appears at least as seductive as the end of a tomcat's tail. The heroine of the piece 'La Moustache' spells out the appeal of this masculine adornment at some length, combining coy suggestiveness and gushing sentimentality with vaguely obscene results:

> Vraiment, un homme sans moustache n'est plus un homme. [...] Une lèvre sans moustache est nue comme un corps sans vêtements [...] le créateur a eu soin de voiler ainsi tous les abris de notre chair où devait se cacher l'amour. [...] Il n'y a point d'amour sans moustaches! [...] Et que d'aspects variés elles ont, ces moustaches! [...] Tantôt elles sont pointues, aiguës comme des aiguilles, menaçantes. [...] Tantôt elles sont énormes, tombantes, effroyables. (7, I, pp. 918-21)

Hair in general frequently suggests sexual desirability, or most memorably, sexual menace, in Maupassant's writing.

The hero of 'La Chevelure' is driven insane when a dead woman's hair is transformed from a macabre keepsake into a haunting succubus. The narrators of the pieces already cited, 'La Femme à barbe' and 'L'Inconnue', are respectively violated and unmanned by hirsute ladies. The frequent references to Duroy's moustache in *Bel-Ami* thus merit attention and are not merely neutral features in his physiognomy.

Mme Walter is immediately drawn to Duroy: 'Il avait la parole facile et banale, du charme dans la voix, beaucoup de grâce dans le regard et une séduction irrésistible dans la moustache. Elle s'ébouriffait sur sa lèvre...' (I, 2). Similarly, Rachel is shown 'levant ses yeux séduits vers la moustache du jeune homme' (I, 4). In the train compartment, Duroy is seen trying to seduce Madeleine, 'promenant doucement, en une caresse énervante et prolongée, sa moustache frisée sur la chair blanche' (II, 1); but later, after submitting, voluntarily, 'elle effleura d'un baiser le bout de sa moustache' (II, 1). In her final efforts to resist Duroy's blandishments in La Trinité, Mme Walter cannot rid herself of the moustache, 'cette image qui hantait ses rêves, qui hantait sa chair, et troublait ses nuits' (II, 4). Duroy's rival Laroche-Mathieu, we learn, has 'une très petite moustache', although its ends are like 'des queues de scorpion' (II, 5). Unsurprisingly, then, when Duroy literally catches him with his pants down, there is a brief confrontation of moustaches – 'Ils étaient face à face, les dents près des dents, exaspérés, les poings serrés, l'un maigre et la moustache au vent, l'autre gras et la moustache en croc' (II, 8) – and Duroy emerges victorious. Such insistent dwelling on this predatory moustache, devouring women's flesh and chewing up a rival, is obviously suggestive. Is the moustache a decent metaphorical substitute for that 'roving penis', which in the nineteenth century usually appears only in pornographic literature? It seems preferable to see it as a sort of ancillary sexual organ, a vital part of the plumage of the seducer, metonymically suggesting masculine potency. Armand Lanoux observes that 'La moustache [...] est une affirmation de virilité quasi exhibitionniste', but at the same time 'A un certain degré de célébrité, la moustache devient un idéogramme' (Dali, Hitler, Stalin, Maupassant...), *48*, p. 276.

The phallus, or phallic emblems, can of course symbolise power in a wider sense than sexual potency. Frequent references to the *bilboquets* at *La Vie française* again create a repetitive pattern which gives an impression of suggestive significance. The toy itself (or 'instrument', I, 3) can be made to seem moderately indecent: the object of the game, played only by men, is to impale the ball on the end of the spike as many times in succession as possible. Forestier is obliged to give his best cup-and-ball to Duroy, since it is too heavy for his flagging arm (I, 6). After his death, Duroy discovers that a joker has lined Forestier's instruments up in order of size in the cupboard with black crepe round the handles, while his own has been adorned with a pink ribbon, marking his succession in Madeleine's bed (II, 2). In addition, Duroy's increasing skill at the game corresponds with his promotion to 'chef des Echos' – 'Car l'adresse au bilboquet conférait vraiment une sorte de supériorité, dans les bureaux de *la Vie Française*' (I, 6). Jean-Louis Bory notes that this corresponds to actual fact: 'La mode du bilboquet faisait alors fureur dans les milieux de la presse française. On raconte que, pour entrer au *Gaulois* d'Arthur Meyer, l'adresse au bilboquet comptait pour la meilleure des notes' (*2*, p. 425). But the *bilboquet* does not seem to be simply an oblique metaphor for sexual prowess or professional virtuosity. Its essentially manipulative nature in any case is more likely to suggest masturbation than fornication (we see six *rédacteurs* lined up in a row, rhythmically tossing their balls up and down, I, 3). Such auto-eroticism is an appropriate symbol for *La Vie française,* an organ which exists to serve the ends of its own members rather than as a genuine means of communication with the public. We have the sense that Duroy is being initiated into the rules of a self-regulating game, as absurd perhaps as the monotonous movement of cup-and-ball.

This sort of symbolism leads us to the more negative aspects of Duroy's relations with others, and the curious femininity of his character which has often been noted. Charles Castella casts him as a sexual man of action: 'c'est bien dans *le geste,* dans *l'acte,* que réside un des secrets de sa réussite; l'acte brutal, déprédateur et conquérant' (*23*, p. 123).

He cites the near rapes of Mme de Marelle in a cab, Madeleine on a train, Mme Walter in a *garçonnière,* and the 'rapt' of Suzanne. It seems doubtful, however, whether such acts of violence make Duroy an 'active hero' and a 'master', as Castella puts it. There is something basically inadequate about his engagement with other people, and women in particular. Jean Borie remarks on

> l'étrange passivité de ce séducteur qui se laisse choisir plutôt qu'il ne choisit, qui ne peut rentrer en rapport avec les hommes que par le vol de leurs femmes, qui maintient avec celles-ci des relations ambiguës dont la brutalité apparente cache mal l'abjecte dépendance où elles le maintiennent. (*21,* p. 52)

Marie-Claire Bancquart sets this argument in a wider context:

> Projection des revanches de Maupassant sur la société, Duroy domine, mais recèle, une tendance qui angoisse l'écrivain, celle d'être *possédé* par la femme et perdu par elle. *Fort comme la mort* et *Notre cœur* nous présentent les vaincus de ce combat, dont Bel-Ami est le vainqueur provisoire. (*4,* p. 29)

Far from being a paragon of unproblematic masculinity, Bel-Ami possesses certain androgynous characteristics. He corresponds, in fact, to the type of 'l'homme-fille' which Maupassant defined in an interesting essay.

'L'Homme-fille' is Maupassant's attempt to create an analytical portrait of a social type in the fashion of La Bruyère's *Caractères,* two years before the appearance of Georges Duroy. 'L'homme-fille' is the being who combines the seductions of masculinity with temperamental qualities that Maupassant regards as typically feminine – charm and capriciousness, effusiveness and insincerity, lack of true moral awareness and exaggerated scrupulousness:

> L'homme-fille est brave et lâche en même temps; il a, plus que tout autre, le sentiment exalté de l'honneur, mais le sens de la simple honnêteté lui manque, et, les circonstances

> aidant, il aura des défaillances et commettra des infamies dont
> il ne se rendra nul compte...   (*7*, I, p. 757)

He is 'la peste de notre pays', and yet 'nous sommes tous, en
France, des hommes-filles' (*7*, I, p. 754). Duroy's affinity
with women of easy virtue is hinted at several times in
Bel-Ami. Apart from the fact that he is effectively kept by
both Madeleine and Mme de Marelle, who presumably lives
in turn off her obliging husband, he is explicitly compared
with a courtesan whom he observes blatantly displaying her
riches from her carriage in the Bois de Boulogne (I, 6):
her audacity seems infinitely preferable to the hypocritical
respectability of the society figures who surround her, and
her success is presented as an anticipatory model for that of
Duroy.

Duroy's own attitude to women contains strong elements
of barely concealed aggression and hostility. If he himself is
'Plus putain que maquereau' (*2*, p. 9), within a few weeks of
his marriage to Madeleine, he is sourly, but significantly,
concluding: 'Toutes les femmes sont des filles, il faut s'en
servir et ne leur rien donner de soi' (II, 2). And indeed, the
misogynous egotist reduces others to mere functional objects
for his own ends. Though this chapter is called 'characters',
most of the discussion so far has concentrated firmly on
Georges Duroy. Few readers are likely to find another character in the book who matches Maupassant's memorable
hero. The critic who asks 'qui ne préférera, malgré tout,
Walter à Georges Duroy, à Laroche-Mathieu, à Madeleine
Forestier?' (*35*, p. 80) seems frankly eccentric. Philippe
Bonnefis states bluntly that, apart from Duroy, the people of
Bel-Ami 'sont à peine des personnages de roman, mais des
utilités plutôt' (*5*, pp. 384-85). In other words, they do not
exist as psychological studies, but rather as devices which
further the narrative movement of the book, as vehicles for
Maupassant's social and historical observation of his age. The
gossip reporter Saint-Potin is a good simple illustration: his
nickname means 'gossip' in fact and thus enshrines his
function in the text. Such utility parts may be just as interesting as potted character portraits in one's study of *Bel-Ami,* as

subsequent chapters will try to show – the critic who complains, for instance, that the morbid poet Norbert de Varenne
is marginal to the book's economy (*23,* p. 130) seems to have
missed an essential point. However, in the concluding pages
of this chapter, it seems worthwhile to look in more detail at
the women characters in the novel, if only to discover what
they reveal about Georges Duroy and his creator.

Bonnefis also argues that 'mise à l'étude, la femme entre
dans la catégorie des objets dont on fait vite le tour'; she is
basically an 'objet de conquête' (*5,* p. 386). Not only does
Duroy use women as rungs on a ladder, but their functional
role in the text is very much that of staging-posts in the
chronicle of Duroy's progression. There are five of them
(omitting Laurine, and minor characters), and it is worth
noting that Duroy seems to behave most viciously towards
them when they begin to assert their own personalities, to
become subjects rather than objects: he is unable to come to
terms with Madeleine's enigmatic, independent assertion of
her political and amorous talents, finds Mme Walter's displays of possessive affection loathsome, and beats up Mme de
Marelle when she offers him a frank assessment of his
behaviour. It is the first and last women in the cycle who
remain the least emancipated: apart from her one outburst,
Rachel never gains any status beyond one of provocative, but
impersonal sexual availability, and whereas Laurine at the
beginning of the novel has a genuine childish charm, Suzanne
Walter at the end of the course in social and sexual exploitation is typecast as a winsome little doll. The women's most
apparent physical and moral characteristics again suggest a
rather schematic stereotyping: Rachel the painted, brazen
hussy, Clotilde de Marelle the bohemian, dark-haired society
woman, the blond-haired *politicienne* Madeleine, the middle-
aged, respectable Mme Walter, white-haired after her en-
tanglement with Duroy, Suzanne, 'un délicieux joujou blanc'
(II, 10), to be passed from father to husband (critics who hope
she will turn out like Nora in Ibsen's *A Doll's House* seem
somewhat optimistic). Duroy's four quarrels with Clotilde de
Marelle about the four other women also perhaps create the

impression of a ritualistic cycle of seduction and rupture where individualised personalities count for little.

Maupassant is rather famous as a misogynist. Feminists who (if they read his work at all) might have their feathers ruffled by his burlesque, but not altogether inaccurate, account of a feminist meeting in 'Les Dimanches d'un bourgeois de Paris', could get their claws into him in revenge by looking at a story such as 'Fou?', where a jealous lover's manic obsession with his mistress's horse barely conceals a degraded and degrading fear of female sexuality. One could compile a *sottisier* of Maupassant's sillier sayings about women, complete with knowing references to Schopenhauer, without much difficulty. But what is perhaps most striking about the treatment of women in *Bel-Ami* is that the dominant female character, Madeleine Forestier, is very much an exception in Maupassant's presentation of women in his fiction.

Just as the sharp-tongued and socially poised Célimène may seem infinitely preferable to the boorish egotist Alceste in Molière's *Le Misanthrope,* on purely personal terms one may find Madeleine Forestier considerably more appealing than the venomous Duroy; she at least combines beauty and talent, unlike her second husband, even if they are equal in their lack of scruples and single-minded social climbing. It is not clear whether Maupassant himself invites us to see Madeleine with much sympathy: she is the only other character in the novel who appears in a mixture of light and shade, perhaps, but her areas of darkness may reflect not so much a perception of the ambivalent richness of human behaviour on the author's part as an inability to reconcile very convincingly the contradictory elements of a personality which he is unable to come to terms with. Normally, Maupassant's sympathetic women figures are socially and sexually marginal: they are marked as inadequate outcasts by society, and by retrieving them the author can cast himself in a humanitarian light without really subverting the ideological and social repression exerted against women by his society. The prostitute Boule de Suif, the potential *demi-mondaine* Yvette, the ungainly spinster Miss Harriet in three of his best stories are seen with genuine pathos, but are also victims of a social and sexual fatality which is presented to us as fixed and inevitable. Madeleine, on the other hand, is hardly a victim, since even if she is obliged to exercise her journalistic and political talents through her husbands and lovers (Forestier, Laroche-Mathieu, Duroy, and finally another journalist, Jean Le Dol), she survives, while two of the men perish, literally in one case, and all of them appear in a somewhat abject position in their relationships. Typically, while Laroche-Mathieu cringes under the bed-clothes during the *constat d'adultère* scene, Madeleine coolly lights a cigarette and asks the police commissioner if he likes his work (II, 8).

This scene, no doubt, is her lowest point. If Duroy betters her here, after he has just pocketed half her inheritance into the bargain, by using a law which allows husbands to punish their adulterous wives, but not, needless to say, wives their adulterous husbands, his victory seems a cheap one. Yet we learn nothing of Madeleine's reaction to these events; she simply vanishes from the scene. Maupassant perhaps lacks the imaginative confidence necessary to pursue a character who is remote from his own scheme of things. It is a straightforward fact about his limitations as a novelist that he was incapable of creating an Anna Karenina or a Dorothea Brooke, although the unhappy Jeanne in *Une Vie* is a passably anaemic version of Emma Bovary. Too often, one feels, he allows Madeleine Forestier to slip away into enigma. Critics remind us (and an eminent Maupassant scholar is himself called Forestier) that *forestiere* means 'stranger, foreigner' in Italian, and that it is a Mme Forestier who unwittingly aids in the downfall of the unfortunate heroine of 'La Parure'. 'La Parure' also gives us a typical comment on womankind:

> les femmes n'ont point de caste ni de race, leur beauté, leur grâce et leur charme leur servant de naissance et de famille. Leur finesse native, leur instinct d'élégance, leur souplesse d'esprit, sont leur seule hiérarchie, et font des filles du peuple les égales des plus grandes dames. (*7*, I, p. 1198)

Elsewhere, the same point is made more trenchantly: 'Chez les femmes, il n'est point de classes. Elles ne sont quelque chose dans la société que par ceux qui les épousent ou qui les patronnent' (*6,* II, p. 99).

Clearly, *Bel-Ami* hardly confirms this judgement, since it is Madeleine who creates Forestier and Duroy, and Duroy who displays the extraordinary chameleon-like adaptability which is perhaps his only true talent. She herself, however, reveals an impressive versatility and resilience for one whose social and emotional background is shrouded in mystery. The character of Madeleine at the very least suggests that Maupassant's attitude to women cannot simply be encapsulated in a few lines as one of patronising chauvinism and latent hostility, even if these elements are unpleasantly predominant in much of his work. It is worth noting in passing that he often writes for a female audience: many of his newspaper articles appeal in the vocative to a 'Madame' presumed to be reading them; Huysmans dismissed the last two novels, *Fort comme la mort* and *Notre cœur,* contemptuously as fit to be set alongside the vapid outpourings of Paul Bourget on the shelves of the Jewish society ladies for whom they were written.

Critics are in fact divided in their assessment of Madeleine Forestier. Parmée comments unfavourably on 'her insatiable desire to pull the strings of power behind the scenes' (*3,* p. 17), while Castella sees her claim to independence within marriage as far from authentic:

> En effet, pour cette intrigante, les rapports amoureux, en dedans et en dehors du mariage, ou du moins leur manifestation sexuelle, représentent une simple monnaie d'échange pour obtenir certains avantages d'ordre économique et social. [...] En outre, femme de tête, qui dissocie amour et mariage, elle est en même temps une sentimentale qui élève l'amour vrai au-dessus du désir charnel. (*23,* p. 138)

It is certainly hard to reconcile her initial rejection of Duroy's overtures and idealised vision of love as a communion of souls (I, 6) with her apparently purely mercenary relationships with Vaudrec and Laroche-Mathieu, or still more with the strictly regulated, impersonal timetable she imposes when married to Duroy:

Elle vivait de son côté, et elle avait l'air de l'aimer beaucoup,
aux heures destinées à l'amour, car elle n'admettait pas qu'on
dérangeât l'ordre immuable des occupations ordinaires de la
vie.   (II, 5)

A rare occasion on which we gain a glimpse of her inner
feelings is during the honeymoon trip to Rouen, when she is
temporarily thrown off balance by the confrontation with
Duroy's uncouth peasant parents and is seized by primeval
panic, a sense of overwhelming solitude, in the forest at
Canteleu (II, 1). Here too we learn that she was an orphan,
whose mother died in destitution and whose father she never
knew. Such details perhaps explain her yearning for an
unrealisable love, as well as her readiness to submit to
successful males for whom love is merely a form of expe-
diency.

   In an interesting, speculative article, James F. Hamilton
highlights such shadowy details in an attempt to provide a
global interpretation of Madeleine's character. The problem
is that Hamilton tends to provide categorical answers to
questions which are at best only hinted at. Thus: 'The
castrative potential of Madeleine is suggested by an image of
her smoking in the early dictation scene' (*41*, p. 328). For
better or worse, there is not really enough evidence in the text
to allow an analysis of this character's 'identity crisis' which
does not appear a little fanciful. Hamilton's comments on
Duroy's own protracted identity crisis as the second 'Monsieur Forestier' seem much more convincing, largely because
the portrait of Duroy is so much more complete. But it is
preferable to discuss the curious triangular formations in the
Forestier household in the next chapter, since they are as
much an example of patterned devices contributing to the
structure of the novel as of psychological investigation of
various permutations of the 'ménage à trois'. Perhaps this
discussion of character could end on a more positive note
with Chantal Jennings's observation that Madeleine Forestier
is 'le seul personnage de *Bel-Ami* qui soit véritablement et
sincèrement désintéressée dans l'exercice du métier qu'elle
aime' (*45*, p. 578). Unfortunately, this view is far too indul-

gent, since journalism as presented in *Bel-Ami* is anything but sincere and disinterested. Rather like the young Colette with her first husband Willy, Madeleine also allows her husbands to take the credit for her work. Is this merely due to the social pressure which restricted women journalists to purely female matters? One of the most famous political and polemical journalists of the 1880s and 1890s was in fact a woman, Séverine, whose subsequent lapse into obscurity is a cruel reflexion on the ephemeral nature of her medium. All in all, it is difficult to avoid the conclusion that in his character portraits in *Bel-Ami* Maupassant has given us a well-stocked gallery of rogues.

3

Structures

'PARIS était bloqué, affamé et râlant.' This memorable alexandrine is the opening sentence of Maupassant's story 'Deux amis', which is quoted because it has attracted what is probably the most radical study of narrative discourse in Maupassant, A. J. Greimas's *Maupassant: la sémiotique du texte. Exercices practiques* (*39*). What we have in Greimas's book is an extraordinarily elaborate reading of the ways in which a piece of narrative conveys its meaning to the reader, or rather a making explicit of the ways in which a reader gives sense to a literary text by responding at a semi-conscious level to the codes and conventions which establish its structure and existence as a work of fiction. Rather like Roland Barthes's famous analysis of Balzac's story 'Sarrasine' in *S/Z*, Greimas's investigation is carried out through a process of segmentation and taxonomy. A sort of inventory of the semiotic features of the story is drawn up in twelve 'sequences', rather in the manner of an anthropologist establishing the grammar of some unknown tribe's language, or a Martian confronting a work of literature for the first time and trying to explain in scientific terms features which remain invisible by their familiar obviousness to the ordinary reader. Clearly, the specificity of a seven-page story is likely to explode when it is submitted to a reading which lasts 267 pages. While Maupassant's text is 'd'apparence simple' and 'légèrement fané' (*39*, p. 10), Greimas's own style seems to tend naturally towards abstraction, jargon and complexity. 'Deux amis', presented with a certain condescension as the 'produit d'un écrivain passablement démodé' (*39*, p. 10), is largely a pretext for an analysis whose details can only really be appreciated by professional semioticians, despite the didactic ring of Greimas's subtitle.

To claim that only the 'professional' reader of, say, Flaubert has the right to hold forth about *Trois contes* and that amateurs are bound to produce mere half-truths and over-rehearsed banalities, is an arrogant piece of academic imperialism, calculated to infuriate the general reader and intimidate the student who is constrained to give utterance about literary texts in pursuit of a degree. Philip Larkin may have gained notoriety in dictionaries of quotations by saying that 'books are a load of crap' (and critics no doubt flies feeding on the dung-heap of literature) but he also reminds us, in an essay called 'The Pleasure Principle', that the study of literature is not some grim experiment carried out with scientific rigour by a team of experts and their juvenile assistants, but a pleasurable experience, an intense form of communication between individual readers and writers. Nevertheless, even if one does not need to be a motor mechanic to drive a car, a few driving lessons are probably indispensable. A 'critical guide' is, one hopes, not just a convenient short-cut for the student too lacking in energy or self-confidence to read a celebrated literary text in a foreign language and form his own judgements about it, but a reading which will illuminate areas of a work which might otherwise remain in darkness for the relatively uninitiated reader. Similarly, it seems foolish to avert one's gaze discreetly from works of literary theory which are intellectually menacing but also potentially enlightening.

Nevertheless, most readers of realist fiction probably want something a lot more concrete than a reading which converts Zola's novels into 'le texte zolien', at the expense of biographical and historical referentiality. To return to Maupassant, one needs to know that the first sentence of 'Deux amis' refers to the siege of Paris during the Franco-Prussian War, and that its twelve syllables are perhaps a parodic yet respectful allusion to Victor Hugo's account in verse of *L'Année terrible* (*7*, I, p. 1512). But at the same time, some conception of what is implied by the 'semiotics of the text' is also vital – in other words, an understanding that a piece of fiction

is primarily a system of linguistic signs and literary conventions, a patterned structure whose meaning is read out of it by
a reader as he converts its codes into characters, plot, themes,
and so forth. A more conscious awareness of the way in
which a novel functions as a system ought to enhance one's
ability to perceive and appreciate the details which combine
to create the intricate richness of a great literary text yet
which tend to remain transparent to the inexperienced
reader.

If this chapter is called structures in the plural, it is to
indicate that more is intended by this heading than the
construction of the plot of *Bel-Ami.* That the novel is divided
into two parts of equal length, the first ending with a death,
the second with a marriage, that there is a noticeable change
in tempo between the two parts, that the book opens with
Duroy heading aimlessly in the direction of the Madeleine
and closes with him having arrived there purposefully – such
features, some of which have already been noted, certainly
show that the action of *Bel-Ami* is not built on a random
series of episodes but conveys a sense of patterned rhythm
and intentionality. But many other aspects of the book also
prove on investigation to have a function in establishing the
patterns which hold together positive and negative in the
chronicle of a progression where success is both glorious and
a fake barely concealing personal and social corruption and
mediocrity, where personal identity is equally flimsy, where
as money proliferates it seems less and less to serve as a
means of satisfying authentic desires and appetites. Certain
key episodes and themes demand attention by virtue of their
repetitive or insistent nature: those mirrors in which Duroy
and others are constantly reflected; the configurations formed
by certain characters around Duroy; the constant references
to money, and the descriptive set pieces carefully placed
throughout the book, both of which are important in creating
its realist texture; that final scene with its apparent apotheosis of the *arriviste,* contrasting with earlier passages of gloomy
nihilism, and yet other passages where the reality principle
seems to succumb to a comic impression of fantastic wish
fulfilment.

It may be, of course, that such episodes do not always form an entirely integrated whole. One critic would have us believe that Maupassant elaborates his picture of worldly success, with its careful reference to historical reality, its air of autobiographical complicity, only to tell us that it is all a mirage: 'the most convinced victim of deceit is Duroy himself', for 'success is only self-delusion and the natural state of man would appear to be failure' (*32*, pp. 163, 164). What is certainly interesting is that *Bel-Ami* does on the surface appear to reverse the account of frustration, humiliation and defeat which is the dynamic of many of Maupassant's most famous stories ('Boule de Suif', 'Miss Harriet', 'La Parure') or for that matter of many of the other novels. If one accepts another critic's view, this contrast between *Bel-Ami* and other works is indeed purely superficial, for Parmée argues that in this novel too, 'as a counterbalance and a sort of poetic justice, Maupassant takes pains to underline the basic futility of ambition. Success is ultimately futile because of the ephemerality of all life' (*3*, p. 20). Charles Castella complains rather oddly about the world-weary poet Norbert de Varenne that 'ce personnage aristocratique ne joue qu'un rôle marginal dérisoire, sans aucune prise sur la structure de l'œuvre' (*23*, p. 130), when this character's marginality and loss of vitality seem precisely intended to promote the message that Dugan and Parmée consider to be central to the book. The exposition of Norbert's views is placed in Chapter 6 of part I, before Duroy's success has really taken off, and before Duroy has had his own intimations of mortality on the night before the duel and at Forestier's deathbed. Norbert's pessimism is summed up in his observation that 'Vivre enfin, c'est mourir!' (I, 6); life is a hill whose summit one reaches at one's peril, since on the descent one realises that the solitude and gradual annihilation of each individual are the only true governing forces of existence; intelligence and consciousness are a curse, since they only reinforce one's awareness of these overwhelming material realities. But Norbert also points out that this litany of gloom has little personal reality for those who, like Duroy, have yet to reach the top of the hill, and indeed, immediately after this lengthy tirade, Duroy goes home in a state of joyous, hopeful intoxication.

It is interesting that this lament echoes most strongly half-way through the book, when Duroy does briefly experience 'la terreur de ce néant illimité' (I, 8) beside Forestier's corpse, but again immediately converts it into an expression of desire for Mme Forestier. Far from being futile, ambition seen in such a context may seem to be a fundamental expression of individual vitality, a life-enhancing force which, whatever its immorality in conventional terms, counteracts the encroaching presence of death and despondency. While waiting for Mme Walter in the church of La Trinité, Duroy notices a woman on the verge of destitution seeking consolation in prayer, and is once more driven to metaphysics, judging creation in the bathetic utterance 'Comme c'est bête tout ça' (II, 4). Unlike this 'pauvresse' passively invoking some 'là-haut', Duroy actively fulfils his wishes by himself: it seems absurd to suggest that two such disparate characters, one showing the mentality of the Christian slave, the other a wolf-like rapacity, should ultimately be equated as 'failures' under the eye of eternity. Though it is true that Maupassant does clearly plant scenes in the book which are meant to create a context where success appears as a form of Pascalian 'divertissement', at the same time, for Maupassant ('l'homme sans Dieu' as Pierre Cogny calls him), such *divertissements* are all we are likely to enjoy: Duroy is a more powerful demi-god for a materialistic age than Jesus Christ and his servants. Mme Walter's pious antics in La Trinité seem as dubious as Duroy's cynical pretence of passion, and she is soon ready enough to submit to him. Once again, then, negative does not simply cancel out positive, but creates an ambivalent pulse of alternating currents – the ephemeral can provide a source of value which holds eternity at bay.

It is surely a reflexion of the skill which Maupassant reveals in the construction of *Bel-Ami* that the reader is led to engage in this sort of debate as much by the juxtaposition of contrasting episodes in the novel as by explicit comment by the narrator. In any case, as was suggested earlier, Maupassant's narrative position is largely neutral, and we are more

likely to suspect covert complicity with Duroy than condem-
nation of him. Another commentator again curiously under-
estimates the tightness of the book's composition when he
remarks that 'all the episodes dealing with Georges's parents
appear to be irrelevant' (*24,* p. 111). In fact, just as we are
reminded of mortality half-way through the book, so too we
are introduced to Duroy's parents (II, 1), who similarly serve
as an ambiguous gauge against which to measure their son's
ascent and triumph. Duroy of course lies about his family
background to his Parisian associates. He tells Mme de
Marelle he was 'élevé dans un château à la campagne' (I, 7),
when in fact his parents are peasants who run a humble café
near Rouen, presumably the seat of his future barony – as it
happens, Maupassant's mother is presumed to have had his
birth certificate forged to make it appear that the writer
himself was born in a Norman château. The distance he has
travelled in class, dress and speech is shown when his parents
fail to recognise him. A comment on Duroy's separation from
authentic rustic values? In fact, Maupassant is rarely sentimental about peasants, who usually appear as cunning, grasp-
ing brutes, fitting ancestors for Duroy, the 'paysan parvenu'
par excellence. Nor does he really betray his background, for
even if he disguises it and maintains his distance from his
parents, in the purely practical terms which govern sentimental relations in the Duroy family, he expresses a degree of
gratitude that seems exceptionally generous (given his normal
behaviour) by sending them 50,000 francs, or at least plan-
ning to do so (II, 10). The episode at Canteleu is thus far from
irrelevant, as once again we are given a marker with which to
judge Duroy, as well as certain images of nature to contrast
with the urban space in which he normally moves.

It is hard to quarrel with Delaisement's opinion that
'*Bel-Ami* est le roman le plus achevé, le mieux composé de
Maupassant' (*28,* p. 228). In some ways, the construction of
the novel is almost too neat, as Duroy's progress is sche-
matically presented in a series of clearly defined steps, which
as Delaisement has cleverly demonstrated (*31*) can easily be
represented diagrammatically, not only in terms of financial,
professional, and sexual success, but also topographically,

since his changes of address are an important feature of his
conquest which is denoted spatially as well as temporally. He
begins on the fifth floor of a sleazy six-storey tenement on
the rue Boursault overlooking the Batignolles railway tracks
(this station, which no longer exists, was near Saint-Lazare) –
the top floors of such buildings of course being reserved for
the impecunious, as they still are in Paris today. He then
moves to the ground-floor *garconnière* rented by Mme de
Marelle on the rue de Constantinople (I, 7); by descending to
street level, he rises socially to some extent, but this sort of
small apartment serves largely for clandestine sexual encounters, so Duroy has really only penetrated a *demi-monde,*
particularly as it is never very clear whether Duroy or Mme
de Marelle pays the rent (II, 10). The move to Mme Forestier's apartment on the rue Fontaine (II, 2) is much more
prestigious: Duroy now becomes Du Roy, and acquires a base
which, largely thanks to Madeleine's skills, becomes a centre
for the political and financial machinations which predom-
inate in the second half of the book. Nevertheless, although
Madeleine's salon collects members of the Cabinet (II, 5), the
real power base remains with Walter (he and Laroche-
Mathieu have been using Duroy as a dupe), whose acquisi-
tion of the prince de Carlsbourg's *hôtel* on the rue du
Faubourg-Saint-Honoré reflects the triumph of high finance
over a decaying aristocratic order. Duroy is intimidated by
the bourgeois comforts of Forestier's home – a lackey better
dressed than he is, an armchair which enfolds him luxurious-
ly (I, 2) – but such comforts pale against the ostentatious
opulence which Walter exhibits to high society and its den-
izens. Yet at the end of the novel, we can assume that Duroy
too will gain permanent access to the Faubourg-Saint-Honoré,
thanks to his capture of Suzanne Walter.

Duroy's progress at *La Vie française* also overlaps closely
with his sexual conquests: there are five women and he has
five different jobs in the course of the novel. He begins as a
clerk in a railway office, earning 1,500 francs a year. The
chroniqueur Jacques Rival earns 30,000 francs a year for two
articles a week: we do not need to struggle to convert 1880s
francs to 1980s pounds to appreciate this twentyfold differ-

ence. Both Forestier and Rachel offer new possibilities to him (he had been thinking of becoming a riding-master in a riding-school – a fatal mistake, in Forestier's view, for such a position would condemn him to servility), and, in a comic revenge scene, Duroy abandons his office (I, 4). Maupassant himself suffered for nearly ten years in lowly positions at the Naval and Education Ministries. But these possibilities in turn lose their appeal: after two months, 'il se sentait enfermé dans ce métier médiocre de reporter, muré là-dedans à n'en pouvoir sortir' (I, 5). Mme de Marelle becomes his mistress, however, and though Madeleine rejects his overtures, her advice to pay court to Mme Walter brings a rapid reward: Duroy is promoted to his third position as 'chef des échos' and invited to dinner by Mme Walter (I, 6). He commands a lavish salary of 1,200 francs a month, and one-third of the way through the novel money thus ceases to serve basic material needs. Duroy's assumption of the *rédaction politique* at *La Vie française* (II, 2) follows naturally on the disappearance of Forestier and the conquest of Madeleine, just as his final promotion to *rédacteur-en-chef* (II, 10) is concomitant with his marriage to Suzanne.

One of the secrets of the readability of *Bel-Ami* is surely that the reader is given a strong sense of movement, of thrusting advancement through such boldly emphasised, inter-linked steps; while the first half of the book concentrates on Duroy's struggles and setbacks, after his marriage to Madeleine there is a shift in the reality principle that controls his success, as the sums of money which Duroy deals with become too large to be related to immediate personal desires and he himself is no longer an individual *arriviste* but a player in a wider political game, a game which will be considered in the next chapter. The novel moves both in a vertical plane and from a small to a larger scale. Yet some critics still argue that all this is illusory: according to Richard B. Grant, Duroy is like the acrobat who looks rather like him at the Folies-Bergère in Chapter 1, dexterously poised in a void; 'life's path is really on a horizontal plane, despite the illusion of rise' (*38*, p. 749). Such a judgement ignores the sheer weight of the concrete details just outlined, and over-emphasises the significance of the void whose presence we glimpse from time to time – even Norbert de Varenne presents life's course as a parabola. It may be that one finds the neat pattern of success somewhat crude or melodramatic: Forestier's early remark that 'Un homme un peu malin devient plus facilement ministre que chef de bureau' (I, 1) has a facile ring to it, though Duroy proceeds to illustrate the point in the rest of the book.

Most commentators agree that money plays a vital role in this pattern: thus for Castella, 'dans *Bel-Ami,* l'argent constitue la substance même de l'univers romanesque' (*23,* p. 100). Certainly the reader is unlikely to forget the obsessive counting of coppers and computations of future resources which bulk so large in the opening chapters of the novel, or the role of the twenty-franc piece in Duroy's exchanges with Mme de Marelle. Duroy experiences intense frustration, rather than actual poverty or deprivation. Maupassant had little real understanding of the latter: blinkered by his own experience, he maintained that a *petit employé* suffered harsher conditions than a miner (*6,* II, p. 279), and he was incapable of stepping outside his own skin into a totally alien environment in the way Zola does in *Germinal* – though he certainly understood suffering, as a grim account of watching over a peasant woman and girl dying of diphtheria in the travel book *Sur l'eau* amply demonstrates. Money at first has an almost organic function – it buys food, drink, the clothes which make a new man, and is highly tangible, to be grasped in the waistcoat pocket as a reassuring presence. The insistent stating of prices (particularly of meals) obviously reflects a certain anxiety, or even anguish, to which expenditure brings a relief carefully proportional to its size: Duroy's initial one franc fifty dinners encapsulate the grimly circumscribed life he is leading, whereas the vast meal to which he and the Forestiers are treated by Mme de Marelle in the aptly named Café Riche (I, 5) is as significant in its price (130 francs – the equivalent of over a hundred cheap lunches) as its menu, for this lavish expenditure is presented as a highly erotic act, as they roll oysters 'semblables à de petites oreilles enfermées en des coquilles' against the tongue, nibble at 'une truite rose comme de la chair de jeune fille', while talking of the other sensual pleasures which such oral indulgence stimulates and anticipates.

Like Maupassant, however, who continued to count the centimes even when dealing in thousands with his publishers, Duroy continues his peasant-like haggling when the necessity to do so has ceased – for example, when proposing to cut down the demand of Vaudrec's nephew for ten per cent of the legacy, or when buying his chronometer from the jeweller (II, 6). He is dissatisfied with the half million francs 'extorqués à sa femme' and viciously envious of Walter ('ce sale juif') and Laroche-Mathieu (II, 7). In an excellent article on 'Maupassant et l'argent', Marie-Claire Bancquart argues that 'l'argent est un *désir*' (*17*, p. 130), but that 'Quand il cesse de correspondre à la satisfaction d'une nécessité physique absolue, l'argent devient désir sur rien, aliénation dans tous les sens du terme' (*17*, p. 135). Maupassant's capitalists are cut off from the organic: in *Mont-Oriol*, the Jewish financier Andermatt is compared to a calculating machine, and lets his wife be impregnated by another man, who in turn abandons Christiane in horror at her pregnancy and takes the daughter of a rich peasant. Walter too is aware of his wife's and daughter's infatuation with Bel-Ami, but responds belatedly only when Duroy becomes a *financial* threat (II, 9). This is why, in Bancquart's view, such figures and the 'milieux sur lesquels ils agissent, [ont] l'allure d'êtres et de milieux irréels, tout en étant parfaitement fondés' (*17*, p. 136). Only Duroy maintains some link with the organic, in his ever renewed relations with Clotilde, which cease to serve a mercenary purpose and thus presumably suggest genuine physical and emotional ties. Otherwise, the world of capitalism is dead, an anti-world 'par rapport à l'univers de la souffrance, du hasard et de la folie dépeint d'autre part par Maupassant' (*17*, p. 138).

The shift in the function of money would thus appear to be both quantitative and qualitative. In fact, money always reflects Duroy's desires, and these desires remain deep-rooted, or rather, since depth is the quality which he precisely lacks, an essential part of his urge to display himself as a social being defined less by his individuality than by his immediate surroundings. He still needs thousands, or millions, to break into politics. But Bancquart is surely right to suggest that there is something hollow about this world, and consequently about *Bel-Ami*'s pretensions as a serious political novel. Rather like those Hollywood gangster movies where 'social comment' is really only part of a glib formula of violence and retribution (the mayor and police commissioner are discovered playing cards with the criminals in a speak-easy), the world of *La Vie française* tends to reduce journalism, politics and finance to an absurd game, symbolised by the *bilboquets* or that early meeting with the team at the newspaper when their crucial editorial conference turns out to be a game of cards (I, 3). And it is significant that those who submit to the organic are eradicated from the team: Forestier dies of tuberculosis, Laroche-Mathieu pays dearly for sleeping with Madeleine.

Returning from the theatre after receiving his share of Vaudrec's legacy, Duroy sees himself reflected with his wife in the flickering light of a match in the full-length mirror on the first-floor landing. 'Voilà des millionnaires qui passent', he says jubilantly. But these are shadowy millionaires: 'Ils avaient l'air de fantômes apparus et prêts à s'évanouir dans la nuit' (II, 6). The first four chapters of the novel cover two months, and the last four ten months. In fact, despite this protracted time sequence, these final chapters give the impression of a madly accelerating tempo. Whereas Duroy is still in an impasse after the first seventy pages of the novel, the last three chapters rapidly pile up within fifty pages the declaration to Suzanne, the jettisoning of Madeleine, the disgrace of Laroche-Mathieu, the divorce, the elopement, the wedding. Is the image in the mirror that precedes this ever tightening spiral of success a comment on its fantastic unreality? Much earlier in the novel, Duroy himself is stunned by the ease with which he succeeds in coupling with Mme de Marelle for the first time in a cab: 'Comme ça avait été facile et inattendu!' (I, 5). The reader too may be surprised, given the constricting clothing worn by both sexes in the period. In this novel which combines a strong sense of social reality with narcissistic wish-fulfilment, where appearance is not exposed by reality but rather makes up new versions of reality, the author's insistent placing of reflexions of the hero and others in mirrors at various points in the story can hardly escape the attention of the careful reader.

Duroy perceives an image of the way he appears to the outside world in his newly hired *parvenu* clothes for the first time in the mirrors on the landings leading to the Forestiers' apartment: three times they reassure him, in fairy-tale manner, that he has in fact become a new man, so different from his original self that he seems to be confronting a stranger: 'il s'était pris pour un autre, pour un homme du monde' (I, 2). The real man, meantime, is at first far from comfortable as he makes his début in a bourgeois salon (he notices the lackey's patent leather shoes are superior to his own footwear), but after the evening passes successfully, he bounds jubilantly down the stairs, until caught out once again by his image:

> il se regarda longuement, émerveillé d'être vraiment aussi joli garçon; puis il se sourit avec complaisance; puis, prenant congé de son image, il se salua très bas, avec cérémonie, comme on salue les grands personnages. (I, 2)

Like Cinderella after the ball, however, Duroy returns to his garret by the railway tracks, with its stagnant odour of stale food, sewage and unwashed humanity. His old clothes are waiting for him on the bed,

> vides, fatigués, flasques, vilains comme des hardes de la Morgue. Et, sur une chaise de paille, son chapeau de soie, son unique chapeau semblait ouvert pour recevoir l'aumône. (I, 3)

Thus Duroy sees himself as other, in images which show him revitalised in his new skin or unable to escape from the deadly embrace of the old skin.

This alternation continues, at least in the first half of the novel. After seducing Mme de Marelle, the next day Duroy first catches sight of her 'au fond du miroir' above the mantelpiece (I, 5); this exchange in the crystalline depths of the glass convinces him that all is well. The last sentence of the novel shows him visualising her adjusting her curls before the mirror: mediation through reflexions thus seems to be an important element in the most successful relationship in the novel. But the opposite pole from this erotic enhancement, with its narcissistic charm, is the mirror which reveals more sinister depths: looking in the glass on the night before the duel, Duroy again fails to recognise himself, for this time what he sees is a corpse, a corpse which then appears stretched out full length on his bed (I, 7), like one of the terrifying doubles which haunt the protagonists of Maupassant's stories. In the second half of the novel, however, externalised images of Duroy seem only to magnify his success – Duroy as millionaire, Duroy as rival to Jesus Christ – even when they have an equally fantastic or hallucinatory quality.

The novel as a genre bound to the mimetic illusion is of course all too often compared to reflecting glass. An epigraph in *Le Rouge et le Noir* tells us, in a famous analogy, that the novel is 'un miroir qu'on promène le long du chemin'; Oscar Wilde observed that the rage of nineteenth-century society against realism was that of Caliban confronting his monstrous image in the mirror. It is thus hardly surprising that the prevalence of references to mirrors in *Bel-Ami* (other instances could have been cited) has excited the attention of commentators. The mirror can be seen as a neutral optical instrument, objectively reflecting the truth, escaping the distorting subjectivity of the beholder. On the other hand, its image which reverses the dimensions of reality and gives the illusion of depth on a plane surface can totally destroy the identity of the self: Lanoux quotes Maupassant himself as saying

En fixant longtemps mes yeux sur ma propre image réfléchie dans une glace, je crois perdre parfois la notion du moi. En ces moments-là, tout s'embrouille dans mon esprit et je trouve bizarre de voir là cette tête, que je ne reconnais plus.   (*48*, p. 258)

It is striking that Bel-Ami's failure to recognise himself usually does not induce a crisis, but allows him to redefine his identity in a favourable way. As Sullivan notes, 'his impulse is not to look inward and analyze but to look outward at his reflected image' (*55*, p. 89), perhaps because the mirror image is removed from the contingencies of time and place and fixes the ephemeral, the cult of appearance which Duroy makes his real self: 'il faut paraître, s'imposer, vivre le mieux possible l'instant, sans souci des tristes lendemains' (*31*, p. 53). Before the duel, the 'lendemain' is too pressingly close to be forgotten so easily; even here, though, Duroy is mainly plagued by the fear he will not *appear* to be courageous.

Unlike his creator and the protagonists of the supernatural stories, possessed by forces outside their control, alienated both from themselves and the world as they struggle against insanity, Duroy is an 'individu non problématique' (*23*, p. 134) whose narcissism reflects his ambition 'd'être un *paraître* parfaitement réussi' (*4*, p. 37). John Raymond Dugan reminds us that the most elaborate mirror in Maupassant's fiction is the three-panelled one in his last novel *Notre cœur,* where the sterile beauty Michèle de Burne, preserving her body uncontaminated from organic exchange with the other, contemplates herself in narcissistic rapture as a sort of living statue. Here the mirror 'embodies the character of the heroine' (*32*, p. 111), who, rather like Bel-Ami, uses others only to sustain this image of herself, as the hero of *Notre cœur* discovers to his cost. A character in Marcel Aymé's novel *Aller retour* (1927), who has spent all his life as a wretched clerk, bitterly regrets that he has never known the values of love, friendship and sincerity. A similar figure in Maupassant's story 'Promenade', which in one descriptive passage overlaps with *Bel-Ami* (II, 2), hangs himself on making the same discovery. But Duroy with his ruthless egocentricity seems incapable of communicating with others except when exploiting them: in other words, he attempts to use people as mirrors to enhance the image which he presents to the world. The violence which is a constant factor in his relations with women reflects a fear of losing his identity, whether through the cloying possessiveness of Mme Walter, the outspokenness of Mme de Marelle, or the superior talent of Madeleine with whom he is reduced to playing 'Monsieur Forestier'.

As has already been noted, Duroy attacks men through their women: when Forestier patronises him, he does not slap him, but resolves to cuckold him (I, 6). While he already inhabits a cosy triangle with Clotilde and M. de Marelle, on his marriage to Madeleine, the cuckold turns out to be Duroy himself. He has supplanted his mentor and rival, as he endlessly points out with his tasteless references to 'ce cocu de Forestier' and the latter's presumed sexual inadequacy, only to find that in the eyes of the outside world he himself is merely a new brand of Forestier. Bonnefis interprets Duroy's friendship with the complaisant M. de Marelle as a 'façon pour lui de neutraliser *l'Autre* (puisque le mari trompé n'en est jamais que l'une des figures), en se l'associant' (*5*, p. 415). But in the configurations he forms with Madeleine, the deceased Forestier, Vaudrec and Laroche-Mathieu, it soon begins to appear that he is the neutralised partner, subordinate both professionally and sexually to the others. The honeymoon period with Madeleine in fact lasts only the length of the chapter which describes the actual honeymoon (II, 1), where she remains submissive in the rural setting, and they share a certain complicity as they promote Duroy's new name and supposed origins. The beginning of the next chapter, however, immediately sweeps away this mood of intimacy: to Duroy's chagrin, he comes home one day with a bunch of roses only to find that the comte de Vaudrec has preceded him with an identical bunch (II, 2); soon Vaudrec on Mondays is followed by Laroche-Mathieu on Tuesdays. In addition, of course, his political articles are largely the work of Madeleine. It is typical of Duroy that he only realises the humiliating situation he is in when colleagues christen him 'Forestier' – derisively acknowledging his chameleon-like adaptation to his new role. It is also significant that Duroy responds, not by doubting his own integrity or competence, but by expressing increasing hostility towards Forestier and

Madeleine – his benefactors, no doubt, but also the mirrors in which his identity is defined and trapped. Thus he struggles at first to distinguish himself from Forestier by emphasising the latter's ludicrous weaknesses, only to realise that it is Madeleine who largely controls his destiny as her husband.

Though Duroy benefits materially from Madeleine's presumed sexual independence (one of the terms of their unwritten marriage pact: I, 8), the more he becomes aware of it, the more threatening he finds it. It has been suggested that Maupassant himself found a character like Madeleine menacingly dominant – she certainly contradicts his 'Schopenhauerian' belief that women have little creative intelligence:

> [elle] représente dans le roman ces femmes calculatrices et intelligentes qui déconcertent, voire irritent Maupassant. [...] Il va de soi que la femme représente pour l'homme-fille un danger: elle lui est trop semblable; elle risque de l'exploiter et de l'émasculer tout à fait. [...] Contre cette aliénation, le seul remède est de garder à la femme – quoi qu'elle veuille – un rôle de reflet.   (*4*, pp. 27-28)

In a piece criticising monogamy, women are compared in a culinary image to dishes of food: for Maupassant,

> n'en garder qu'une [femme], toujours, me semblerait aussi surprenant et illogique que si un amateur d'huîtres ne mangeait plus que des huîtres, à tous les repas, toute l'année.   (*6,* II, p. 333)

Women are objects to be consumed and cannot, of course, enjoy the same relationship with men; widows like Madeleine or divorcees are not attractive because of their experience, but on the contrary are soiled goods, 'une marchandise légèrement défraîchie' (*6,* II, p. 87). In fairness to Maupassant, one should point out that he was at times prepared to acknowledge that such opinions did not have the force of an absolute (his references to Schopenhauer usually look like desperate attempts to support a weak case by leaning on an

inviolable authority), but were largely socially and ideolog-
ically conditioned:

> L'homme, en jugeant la femme, n'est jamais juste; il la
> considère toujours comme une sorte de propriété réservée au
> mâle, qui conserve le droit absolu de la gouverner, moraliser,
> séquestrer à sa guise; et une femme indépendante l'exaspère
> comme un socialiste peut exaspérer un roi.   (6, II, p. 55)

Nevertheless, it remains true that sexual relations in
Maupassant are centred on power, domination and consump-
tion, in which one partner loses his or her autonomy, and
becomes a victim and object (it may be the male as often as
the female). As 'Monsieur Forestier', Duroy is clearly an
object of derision, possessed by this other self: 'l'image de
Forestier était rentrée en son esprit, le possédait, l'étreignait'
(II, 2). The surge of hatred he feels towards Madeleine when
she tacitly admits to deceiving Forestier reveals a vicious
insecurity ('Puisqu'elle avait trompé l'autre, comment pour-
rait-il avoir confiance en elle, lui?', II, 2), but disillusionment
also allows him to escape the trap of surrendering to love and
affection: 'Toutes les femmes sont des filles, il faut s'en servir
et ne leur rien donner de soi' (II, 2), and thus purges the
obsession. Henceforth, he will turn elsewhere in order to
define his identity, merely keeping up a pretence of intimacy
with Madeleine. In the next chapter, he stops the Forestier
joke at the office, is reconciled with Clotilde, and begins
paying court to Mme Walter. Two descriptive details subtly
underline the resolution and outcome of this crisis, which
comes to a head during a carriage ride in the Bois de
Boulogne: two swans fading into the distance perhaps suggest
the breaking of the brief spell of romantic love, while the Arc
de Triomphe yawning up at the gateway to the city, ready to
stride down the Avenue des Champs-Elysées like a lumbering
monster devouring all in its path, offers a grossly magnified
image of Duroy's future course.

These last few pages seem to have brought the discussion
full circle, as we come back again to the ways in which
Duroy's character and success are defined. But the point to

remember is that, however much the personality of Bel-Ami dominates the book, it is created as much by the placing of key themes, episodes or other patterned devices as by explicit psychological commentary. If, as has been argued, most of the characters are largely functional, serving to mark out the steps of Duroy's progress or to provide social and satirical points of reference, one could also suggest that Duroy's own autonomy is highly limited – he has no real 'self', but is an image made up by external forces, riding currents which he can follow but cannot control. Although the final chapter of *Bel-Ami* appears to raise the hero to a mythic level, other elements in the economy of the novel tend to exceed this particular character, making it more than a fictitious biography. The book's nihilistic message is often noted – according to one critic, death is an 'idée obsédante' in this novel (*12*, p. 237). In fact, to recapitulate the argument on this subject, one needs to distinguish the first part of the book from the second: when he resolves his identity crisis with Madeleine, Duroy also shakes off human weaknesses ('Le monde est aux forts. Il faut être fort. Il faut être au-dessus de tout', II, 2), and rejects the 'organic' – the basic problems which assail him in the beginning disappear as he is lifted on the spiral of success. *Bel-Ami* is a pessimistic book not because it tells us, with banal reductivism, that success is meaningless in the face of eternity, but because the world it portrays becomes increasingly inhuman. To the most unsympathetic reader, Duroy may appear to be a puppet caught up in an absurd melodrama. What saves the novel is not the presence of the central character, but rather the presence of a material, tangible reality, which holds the book together both by giving it a strong historical referentiality (as the next chapter will try to show) and by acting as a source of vitality which reanimates the dead world of Duroy's society.

That *Bel-Ami* is a novel which has a strong visual and dramatic appeal is demonstrated by the fact that it has been adapted on several occasions for both theatre and cinema (and also British television). Louis Daquin's film version achieved a certain notoriety, for reasons which will be dis-

cussed in the next chapter. The first theatrical performance
was at the Théâtre du Vaudeville in 1912. A more recent
version was performed at the Théâtre de la Renaissance in
January 1954, apparently arousing none of the controversy of
Daquin's film a few months later. The text of this stage
adaptation by Frédéric Dard (who is more famous as the
creator of 'San Antonio') is printed in *Paris-Théâtre* (March
1954) and makes interesting reading, mainly because it reveals, if only by default, the hidden strengths of Maupassant's
book. At first sight, Dard seems to have been extremely
faithful to the novel, given the ruthless compression needed
to turn its 400 pages into a three-hour play. One realises how
much the novel is built round a core of events of a highly
dramatic nature; obstacles are overcome in ways which are
both unexpected yet also create a patterned progression.
Much of the dialogue is taken directly from the novel.
Transitions between the 'tableaux' are sometimes effected by
a narrator who reads out equivalent transitional passages
from *Bel-Ami* – a modest, if somewhat ponderous, acknowledgement of the authority of the novel. But Dard's omis-
sions, though inevitable, fatally distance his play from the
original: out go minor characters like Laurine, minor episodes like those dealing with Duroy's family background,
and, above all, the sense of space and place which the novel
creates through its descriptive density. Stripped down to the
'essentials', *Bel-Ami* becomes a crude melodrama; Duroy
loses the strongly emphasised connections to a particular
milieu and society which underpin his character, and becomes a caricature of an *arriviste,* a theatrical villain twirling
his moustache.

Dard's play ends with Duroy confronting Mme de Marelle, after his marriage with Suzanne has been agreed. The
last word of the text is 'PARIS!', as Duroy looks forward to his
next conquest, echoing Rastignac's famous challenge to the
city at the end of *Le Père Goriot,* 'A nous deux maintenant!'
This unilinear conclusion, though perfectly appropriate for
this streamlined version of the *arriviste*'s progress, does not
correspond to the ending of the novel itself. Duroy, we recall,

is married in the church of the Madeleine, the vast edifice dominating the areas around the *grands boulevards* in which he has mapped out his victories, looking across the river to the Chamber of Deputies, and suggesting in its evocation of Mary Magdalene, the fallen woman redeemed, that 'l'homme-fille' himself, having jettisoned his own Madeleine, has achieved his particular form of secular redemption. The ceremony is performed by the Bishop of Tangier, fittingly enough, given the importance of the Moroccan venture in the book. He addresses Duroy as an exceptional being, and Duroy himself addresses thanks to God:

> Il se sentait en ce moment presque croyant, presque religieux, plein de reconnaissance pour la divinité qui l'avait ainsi favorisé, qui le traitait avec ces égards.   (II, 10)

Under the gaze of the people of Paris, Duroy, 'affolé de joie, se croyait un roi qu'un peuple venait acclamer' (II, 10). But the last image of the novel is his memory of Mme de Marelle adjusting her curls in the glass; the last word is 'lit' (i.e. 'bed').

This final set piece, unlike the stage version, allows a variety of interpretations. Is Maupassant saying that religion, as much as politics or love, depends on appearances and the ability to bluff one's way to power? Is 'l'Homme-Dieu' fooled by Duroy when he obligingly consecrates his triumph? Religion, as it were, becomes another ally; Duroy's consecration is a matter of pure spectacle, and we are not meant to engage in theological debates about its validity. But is this spectacle a meaningless charade or a genuine triumph? If Duroy's thoughts return to Mme de Marelle, does this suggest that his progress is over, and the sort of regression predicted by Norbert de Varenne is soon to begin, or simply that he still retains a few valid emotions? Marie-Claire Bancquart sees this conclusion as establishing a grim secular myth:

> Duroy est plus fort que le Christ, dont il se sert. Il est l'idéal du nouvel ordre social, pour lequel Dieu n'est plus que référence machinale et morte; c'est l'érotisme et la violence qui le maintiennent sur les flots du monde.   (*4*, p. 37)

François Mauriac, however, takes a more apocalyptic view:

> De ce livre *matérialiste* se dégage avec une irrésistible évi-
> dence la terreur biblique de la pluie de feu. Bel-Ami, dressé
> sur les marches de la Madeleine, dans l'apothéose du dernier
> chapitre, suscite l'ange exterminateur et annonce que les
> temps sont proches ...   (quoted in *27,* p. 87)

Some readers may find the evidence for this sort of Christian
imperialism entirely resistible; but such an interpretation at
least emphasises the rich multiplicity of Maupassant's images
of Bel-Ami.

   Bel-Ami is indeed a materialist novel, and that is perhaps
its lasting virtue. The critic Brunetière rebuked the author
'd'observer des choses qui n'en valent pas la peine'; for
instance that 'la porte des Folies-Bergère est "une porte
matelassée à battants garnis de cuir"...' (*22,* p. 215). The
novel is essentially built round a series of set-piece descriptions, from the opening street scene to the climax in the
church. Many of these have been discussed already, and are
clearly functional, in that they serve as vehicles for key
themes or episodes (Duroy's places of residence, the salons of
Mme Forestier and Mme Walter, two descriptions of the Bois
de Boulogne, the duel, and so forth). It would be tedious and
impractical to examine every single scene and try to justify its
place in the economy of the novel. Why the elaborate
description of a fencing match in Chapter 3 of Part II, for
example? The answer to Brunetière's complaint is that details
are in fact significant by the simple fact of their presence: the
purpose of description in a naturalist novel is to suggest the
overriding presence of the phenomenal world in all its material density. Some of Maupassant's descriptions have a lyrical,
sensual appeal that carries a higher charge than the characters
who move against this supposed background. In the Bois de
Boulogne, however vile its parade of vice and hypocrisy, the
air is 'léger, savoureux comme une friandise de printemps' (I,
6) ('as delicious as fresh bread' in Parmée's translation, *3,*
p. 166). Nature, the outside world, exceed the perspectives of
characters and their egotistical concerns: the sun sets magnif-

icently over the dying Forestier and when Duroy arrives wretchedly for his duel, he finds that

> C'était une de ces rudes matinées d'hiver où toute la nature est luisante, cassante et dure comme du cristal. Les arbres, vêtus de givre, semblent avoir sué de la glace ...   (I, 7)

Reference to the importance of such descriptive passages, which are not just incidental asides, may seem somewhat perfunctory at this stage; but, as we shall see, Maupassant's naturalism is the ultimate source of vitality in *Bel-Ami*.

4

History

T H E extraordinary impact of Zola's *Germinal* is in large part due to the fact that the reader is overwhelmed by the world with which he is confronted, a world both fascinating in its novelty and horrifying in its inescapable suffering and oppression. No essay on mining conditions in the Second Empire could have this effect. Zola's fiction creates a sort of historical transparency: we have the impression that history has been brought to life and embodied in the destinies of the individuals who move through the pages of the novel. George Steiner tells us in *The Death of Tragedy* that tragedy, that eminently literary form, with its man-centred or God-centred metaphysic, cannot deal with the oppressive historical facts of the mid-twentieth century. It is hard to invest industrial-ised slaughter, whether of animals or humans, with much aesthetic dignity. Perhaps this is why the literary works which deal most convincingly with our modern horrors are those which tend towards the narrative neutrality of the documen-tary. Thomas Keneally's *Schindler's Ark* seems infinitely preferable in its re-creation of the harrowing events which overtook central Europe during the Second World War to novels like William Styron's *Sophie's Choice* or D. M. Thom-as's *The White Hotel,* because Keneally's book avoids as far as possible the fictional contrivance, the artistic embroidery which give the impression in the last two cases that history is reduced to a pretext for literary conceits, that suffering is not being redeemed or acknowledged but exploited. There is of course no absolute dividing line between historical and liter-ary representation. Both are forms of narrative which inter-pret experience with varying degrees of contrivance. We tend to read films like *The Battle of Algiers, Missing,* or *The*

Killing Fields as historically true statements about individuals confronted with political realities, the spectator vicariously experiencing fiction as fact, as fiction provides a convenient framework for reflexion on factual events and fact is vitalised through the powerful fictional naturalism of the cinema.

Germinal, then, can be called a historical novel, not simply because it evokes with careful documentary accuracy a world which had passed into history twenty or so years before it was written, but also because it obliges the reader to face certain historical facts relevant to Zola's own age, or any industrial society, to reflect on the ways in which literature can present in a peculiarly effective concrete way the social, political or economic forces which control the lives of individuals, which exceed the merely 'literary', particularly in their most horrifying manifestations, and yet which without literary representation can remain abstractions barely perceptible in day-to-day reality. Zola himself remarked that he wished in *Germinal* to present the issues which would be of vital importance in the twentieth century – notably, the conflict between capital and labour. Maupassant in *Bel-Ami* deals with political issues on a far grander scale than Zola can encompass in the closed world of his miners – the interaction of high finance, journalism and government – yet *Bel-Ami* remains a much smaller novel than *Germinal.*

Bel-Ami is Maupassant's attempt to produce a novel like *L'Education sentimentale,* where fictional individual destinies are set against or linked with the public events of recorded history. Such novels are qualitatively different from, say, *Madame Bovary* or *Pierre et Jean,* which, however revealing they may be about aspects of life in the nineteenth century, focus essentially on invented, private dramas, which may or may not attain a wider typicality. The structure of *Bel-Ami* or *L'Education sentimentale,* on the other hand, depends not simply on the intrinsic components which form a novel but on reference to an external historical reality. One cannot really understand *L'Education sentimentale* without some knowledge of the July Monarchy and Second Republic; *Bel-Ami* will contain a lot of blank spots for the reader unfamiliar with the early years of the Third Republic. More is involved than simple historical asides such as references to the building of the Paris metro, or the colonisation of Algeria and Tunisia. A certain amount of factual information has to be absorbed, if one is to appreciate, for example, the significance of Maupassant's description of the newspaper, *La Vie française,* and its role in promoting the Moroccan campaign. But though such facts cannot be ignored, their ultimate purpose is to help the reader form judgements which are aesthetic rather than historical. One wants to know both what sort of commentary Maupassant is making on history, and how far he has integrated it into the economy of his fiction.

There seems to be little critical consensus about the success of *Bel-Ami* as a political novel. One commentator sees it, somewhat extravagantly, as a 'document extraordinaire sur les réalités économiques de l'époque' (Thérive, quoted in *1,* p. ix, n. 3). Delaisement points out the thinness of Maupassant's portrayal of the world of politics – the picture 'se résume trop souvent dans la concussion élevée en institution d'Etat' (*1,* p. xi) – yet is still prepared to invest the author's analysis with a strong moral force:

> *Bel-Ami* est *un réquisitoire*: le roman condamne cette absence de sens civique, d'honnêteté, de mesure, ce goût immodéré pour l'argent de tous les hommes politiques et, plus encore, un manque absolu de scrupules qui rend vraisemblables toutes les aventures. (*31,* p. 31)

Maupassant as indignant moralist? It is just as easy to see a cynical complicity behind the somewhat complacent recounting of villainy and profiteering. Paul Ignotus, in any case, is sceptical about the seriousness of the account:

> The picture of nation-wide corruption and of a nationalism kept going for big business interests – a vision prompted by the recent adventures of French colonialism in North Africa – is creditably outspoken but naive in details, a Punch and Judy show with the pretence of a sociological study. (*43,* p. 152)

Marie-Claire Bancquart refers more kindly to the 'humour dynamique' of Maupassant's social tableau (*4,* p. 12), but stresses the central importance of current affairs in *Bel-Ami*: 'On ne peut guère imaginer roman qui se réclame davantage de l'actualité la plus proche' (*4*, p. 10). Unfortunately, this sort of *actualité* is likely to be as dead as mutton for the reader looking at the novel from the distance of a century.

For a novel which supposedly denounces the corruption of journalism, *Bel-Ami* is itself strangely embedded in journalism. *La Vie française* is most often said to be based on the newspaper *Gil Blas*: the portrait is hardly flattering, yet *Bel-Ami* was itself serialised in *Gil Blas*. Again, the unscrupulous director of *La Vie française,* Walter, is usually said to be based on Arthur Meyer, Jewish convert and director of *Le Gaulois*. Yet Maupassant sold stories and articles to *Le Gaulois* before and after the appearance of *Bel-Ami*. One should beware of a certain circularity in such identifications: it is slightly disconcerting to turn to the massive *Histoire générale de la presse française* only to find the bland statement, offered with little evidence, that *Bel-Ami* is 'une description romancée de la vie du *Gil Blas*' (*42*, p. 380), since one then suspects that the portrait of *Gil Blas* may be drawn as much from *Bel-Ami* as the reverse. Maupassant's disavowals in 'Aux critiques de *Bel-Ami*' are somewhat coyly disingenuous, since his main aim seems to be to exonerate himself from accusations of maligning his colleagues in the press. Duroy, he avers, is not a 'véritable journaliste': 'il s'est servi de la Presse comme un voleur se sert d'une échelle. S'ensuit-il que d'honnêtes gens ne peuvent employer la même échelle?' If one retorts that this particular ladder is far from being a neutral instrument – a burglar's jemmy might have been a better analogy – Maupassant responds by saying that *La Vie française* is not 'un grand journal, un vrai journal' but 'une de ces feuilles interlopes, sorte d'agence d'une bande de tripoteurs politiques et d'écumeurs de bourses, comme il en existe quelques-uns, malheureusement'. And needless to say, he concludes, 'je n'ai visé personne' (*6*, III, pp. 166-67).

Walter's newspaper, we learn at the beginning of *Bel-Ami*, 'n'a été fondé que pour soutenir ses opérations de bourse et ses entreprises de toute sorte'. Walter is also a deputy (he is a coarser reincarnation of a character like the industrialist and

politician Dambreuse in *L'Education sentimentale*), but the
paper's stance is, to say the least, fluid ('officieux, catholique,
libéral, républicain, orléaniste, tarte à la crème et boutique à
treize', I, 4). It is worth noting that when presenting the
paper's contributors, Maupassant originally named real journalists among them – such as Aurélien Scholl, a star of
Parisian journalism in the 1880s – and then used entirely
fictional names (*1*, p. 61, n. 1; *2*, p. 426). The news which *La
Vie française* prints is highly coded, since it is 'avant tout un
journal d'argent, le patron étant un homme d'argent à qui la
presse et la députation avaient servi de leviers', assisted by a
team 'qui naviguait sur les fonds de l'Etat et sur les bas-fonds
de la politique' (I, 6). The modern reader perhaps needs to be
reminded that the 'Echos', of which Duroy takes control,
have a wider function than a modern gossip column. They
normally appeared on the front page of a newspaper, taking
the form of a series of small items, each of which was 'le bref
commentaire sensé, judicieux, plaisant ou ému d'un fait
politique, artistique, mondain, sportif' (*1*, p. 117, n. 1). The
text tells us that 'C'est par eux qu'on lance les nouvelles,
qu'on fait courir les bruits, qu'on agit sur les public et sur la
rente' (I, 6). The political articles which Duroy subsequently
writes are equally coded. Once Walter's team-mate Laroche-
Mathieu has become Minister for Foreign Affairs, *La Vie
française* 'n'était plus l'organe suspect d'un groupe de tripoteurs politiques, mais l'organe avoué du cabinet' (II, 5), a
voice which is listened to seriously. Duroy's function, to
recall the plot of the novel, is to promote the invasion of
Morocco while making it clear between the lines that it will
not take place. But he does not know, until Mme Walter
reveals the secret, that he has been duped: Walter and
company have been buying up the Moroccan loan surreptitiously, in the knowledge that when the invasion takes place,
the French government will guarantee the Moroccan debt
and their stock will vastly increase in value.

Like Duroy himself, *La Vie française* does not change
intrinsically: its transformation from a marginal journal to a
powerful, respected newspaper can hardly be seen as anything other than a comment on the venality of journalism and

its backers in the Third Republic. How accurate is this picture? If one takes the trouble to look at French newspapers of the 1880s, one is first struck by how different they are from their modern equivalents, particularly in layout and size, but also in the function which they serve. 'News', in the modern sense of the term, does not actually bulk very large. *Gil Blas* in 1885, the seventh year of its publication, has four pages in each issue; each page consists of six uninterrupted columns, unbroken by large headlines. The first page of the number of 1 January contains a story by Armand Silvestre, 'Nouvelles et échos', and 'Nouvelles à la main' (snippets of gossip); page two has political information, *faits divers,* and miscellaneous items; page three is largely taken up by the *feuilleton* of *Germinal*; and page four by advertisements and reports from the Bourse. The appearance of *Le Gaulois* for the same year is very similar; on the whole it contains more political information than *Gil Blas,* however. In both cases, objective presentation of events at home or abroad is minimal, compared with the space devoted to literary pieces, political commentary and gossip. Selling for fifteen centimes (like *La Vie française* in *Bel-Ami*), both *Le Gaulois* and *Gil Blas* had circulations which seem tiny nowadays (14,854 and 28,257 copies daily in July 1880, according to *42*). The *petite presse* (the equivalent of the smaller format of a modern tabloid) at five centimes reached a far wider audience: *Le Petit Journal* sold over 500,000 copies daily in the same period. But pictures of the front page of *Le Petit Parisien* in 1880 and 1910 reveal the radical transformation of all newspapers as they entered the twentieth century: in 1880, we still have the *feuilleton* at the bottom and a long *chronique* above; whereas in 1910, there are large headlines crossing the columns, photographs, and articles devoted to news items like the flooding of the Seine (see *42*).

To look at the Parisian press in the 1880s is, in other words, very much to enter a foreign country. Nevertheless, this sort of brief factual survey should already suggest that the closed, manipulative world of *La Vie française* in *Bel-Ami* does seem to correspond accurately to real newspapers produced for a small audience which lived in a world yet to be

opened up by mass communications, and which required
specific literary, political or financial information in its
reading of the press. Circulation was of little importance to
the influence of newspapers which operated within a small
circle of power:

> Un des rôles, et souvent la fonction essentielle, de la plupart
> des petits journaux d'opinion, mais aussi de bien des feuilles à
> grand tirage, était de donner à leurs directeurs politiques,
> députés ou sénateurs, un moyen de participer au jeu politi-
> que, aux intrigues pour la conquête des portefeuilles dont les
> Chambres étaient le théâtre.   (*42*, p. 253)

The press law of July 1881 greatly reduced the legal formal-
ities for publishing a newspaper. The press in the Third
Republic, freed from financial threat by the removal of the
cautionnement and stamp duty, and the censorship which
under the Second Empire led to the frequent closure of
newspapers and prosecution of journalists who expressed
controversial views (witness the case of Jules Vallès), could
become 'l'instrument ou le reflet de toutes les grandes luttes
politiques et sociales' (*42*, p. 23). But the situation was still far
from rosy. The notorious 'lois scélérates' of 1893 and 1894,
introduced after a series of terrorist outrages, established
draconian penalties for those who uttered opinions which
were even mildly libertarian. And the other side of the coin of
relative press freedom was widespread corruption:

> A la limite, bien des campagnes de presse, même dans les plus
> grands journaux, frisaient le chantage et la vénalité de la
> presse était une tare dont peu de journaux de la période furent
> exempts.   (*42*, p. 361)

A book published in 1895, significantly entitled *Les
Coulisses de la presse: mœurs et chantages du journalisme,*
confirms such judgements. The author comments for example on the dubious nature of the *échos* column of *Gil Blas*:

> Cette rubrique est le Bottin et l'indicateur du monde de la
> galanterie, l'annoncier des scandales conjugaux, le moniteur

des maisons de rendez-vous et l'album-réclame des filles tari-
fées dont l'intérêt est d'être le plus souvent citées pour obtenir
ainsi une cote élevée dans les maisons de tolérance du quartier
de la Madeleine ou des Champs-Elysées.   (*46*, p. 260)

The 'dossier Aurélien Scholl' in the archives of the Préfecture
de police in Paris reveals that this notable journalist had
convictions for assault, indecent behaviour, libel and suspicion of embezzlement (*4*). Maupassant's observation in his
defence of *Bel-Ami* that 'voulant analyser une crapule, je l'ai
développée dans un milieu digne d'elle afin de donner plus
de relief à ce personnage' (*6,* III, pp. 166-67) thus seems
entirely justified, even if, as he says, he has concentrated on a
particularly dubious type of newspaper and has no pretension
of providing a synthesis of all the Parisian press in *La Vie
française*.

Nevertheless, as Jean-Louis Bory remarks, *Bel-Ami* shows
how the press 'devient un état dans l'état, parce qu'elle se
dresse au carrefour, vital en démocratie, où se rencontrent
politique, finance et opinion publique' (*2,* pp. 13-14). Maupassant himself describes the press as 'une sorte d'immense
république qui s'étend de tous les côtés' (*6,* III, p. 165). At
this stage in the discussion, then, one can accept that Maupassant's picture of *La Vie française* is both elaborated in
some detail and relatively authentic. It seems advisable to
look briefly at the political events referred to in the novel,
before considering how far the text itself provides a valid
commentary on the history of the writer's age, and how far
such elements are successfully integrated into the text.

References to North Africa are of course scattered through
the novel from the first chapter, when we learn that Duroy
spent two years there as a soldier. His first article recounts his
memoirs of this time. While the *sous-officier* Duroy initially
exploits Arabs on a small scale, the Moroccan expedition in
the second half of the book is a financial enterprise making
millions for Walter, and indirectly for his future son-in-law
Duroy. We learn very few details about this expedition: it is
passed over in a sentence – 'Depuis deux mois la conquête du
Maroc était accomplie' (II, 7) – while pages are devoted to

describing how Walter spends his ill-gotten gains from this venture. Both politics and the press are in fact subordinate to money-making in *Bel-Ami*. Histories of the Third Republic in the 1880s – the era of 'Opportunism' – do nothing to invalidate Maupassant's picture. Financial scandals and shady dealing seem to have been rife. Walter's gang of speculators in the Chamber of Deputies invites comparison with such notorious figures as the deputy Daniel Wilson (son-in-law of President Jules Grévy), whose trafficking in decorations forced Grévy's resignation in 1887. The failure of the Panama Canal Company in 1889 was to expose the most celebrated scandal of the period before the Dreyfus Affair, when large numbers of deputies, ministers and senators were suspected of being 'chéquards', receivers of substantial bribes. The sort of 'tripotages véreux' of which Walter is suspected as the 'patron d'une banque louche' (II, 7) are perhaps illustrated in Maupassant's own time by the collapse of the Catholic bank, the Union générale, at the beginning of 1882, when thousands of small savers were ruined while Jewish and Protestant financiers benefited from their rival's loss, which they are often alleged to have engineered. Opponents of the government on both left and right denounced the colonialist ventures of the period (in Egypt, Tonkin, Tunisia) as pretexts for individual commercial gain and for distracting attention from France's humiliation in Europe ten or fifteen years before by Germany.

Maupassant himself knew North Africa well, as his newspaper articles (often critical of government policy) show; such articles were also used in the elaboration of the travel books *Au soleil* (1884) and *La Vie errante* (1890). Morocco did not in fact become a French protectorate until 1912: not only is the African scene distant (despite the author's personal knowledge) in *Bel-Ami,* but historical reality is also transposed. Tunisia, of course, was occupied by a French expeditionary force in 1881 and became a French protectorate in the same year. When one learns that after the invasion, France guaranteed the Tunisian debt and the *obligations* issued to cover it immediately rose in value, having been surreptitiously bought up in advance by backers of the expedition (the journalist Henri Rochefort was unsuccessfully prosecuted for denouncing such dishonest speculation in *L'Intransigeant*), it is hard to avoid the assumption that the fictitious Moroccan campaign in *Bel-Ami* is a pointed re-enactment of the Tunisian venture. Thus André Vial states that the plot of the novel 'constitue de bout en bout une transposition, au compte du Maroc [...], des événements de Tunisie' (*60*, p. 323). Why the change? 'Ce n'était que par prudence', observes another commentator (*18*, p. 135). Such statements somewhat oversimplify the matter: Maupassant does in fact refer directly to the Tunisian campaign in *Bel-Ami*, at least three times (II, 3, 4, and 5). The third reference explicitly tells us that

> le nouveau cabinet ne se pourrait tenir d'imiter l'ancien et d'envoyer une armée à Tanger, en pendant de celle de Tunis, par amour de la symétrie, comme on met deux vases sur la cheminée.   (II, 5)

'Transposition' is perhaps a misleading description of what is actually an *elaboration* or extension of actual historical events. Bory suggests that by such inventions, 'Maupassant a voulu serrer de plus près l'actualité politique, tout en renonçant à la vérité historique' (*2*, p. 430). Just as his characters allude to real people, without simply being disguised portraits, so too Maupassant's presentation of events patently alludes to the political atmosphere of the 1880s without simply transposing real events into fiction. By grafting Morocco on to Tunisia, he allows himself a certain distance from reality, a degree of fictional autonomy.

Marie-Claire Bancquart recapitulates the chronology of the novel in her excellent edition of *Bel-Ami*. The novel begins, she claims, on 28 June 1880 and ends on 20 October 1883; the action lasts three years and four months. She also points out that it is quite unlikely that Duroy could have obtained a divorce within three months. One could add that it is even more unlikely than that, since by her reckoning he is divorced in 1883, while divorce was re-introduced only in July 1884. But the essential point is that while it is quite easy to establish the internal chronology of the novel, thanks to the author's habit of dating many significant events (which suggests again the careful construction of the plot), there is never any reference to the precise year in which the action takes place. All we know is that Duroy spent two years in Africa from 1874 onwards, and five years in the army. He has been in Paris for six months when the story begins. If the first year was 1879, the Moroccan expedition would take place in autumn 1881 (six months after the Tunisian campaign was initiated). All we can really say, however, is that the novel is firmly set in the early 1880s.

Maupassant may well have given us an accurate, authentic image of the political corruption of the Third Republic in *Bel-Ami,* where invention skilfully runs parallel to and comments on reality. But, as has already been suggested, this does not mean that his understanding of politics is very deep or that *Bel-Ami* carries much conviction as a political novel (if a Catholic novel reveals that human destiny is subject to unseen spiritual forces, a political novel ought to give us a corresponding sense of how individuals are caught up in a historical socio-economic process, the prey of unseen material forces). The basic problem seems to be that Maupassant despises politicians and all those who associate with them. Thus Laroche-Mathieu is presented as

> un de ces hommes politiques à plusieurs faces, sans convictions, sans grands moyens, sans audace et sans connaissances sérieuses, [...] sorte de jésuite républicain et de champignon libéral de nature douteuse, comme il en pousse par centaines sur le fumier populaire du suffrage universel.   (II, 2)

He is summed up as a 'beau garçon bien coiffé'. 'Quels crétins que ces hommes politiques!' thinks the envious Duroy (II, 5), and if one looks at Maupassant's newspaper articles on the subject, one cannot help concluding that he largely shares this view.

His position towards political and economic events is probably intended to convey the impression that he is a sceptical and independent critic of current affairs, who does not participate in the game but knows all the dirty tricks the players use. In fact, his independence all too often amounts to little more than facile cynicism, and his impartiality to a refusal to give a serious analysis of a situation. A modern reader, for example, will find an article on the Union générale affair far too elliptical to be very informative; once again, the public has been conned, but Maupassant's remark 'J'avoue qu'il y a dans ces mots: *affaires de Bourse, spéculation, un mystère impénétrable pour mon esprit*' reveals beneath its sarcastic disdain an irritating indifference to the causes of the crash ('A qui la faute?', *6*, I, p. 393). He is too ready to reduce politics to the level of a game of Monopoly. The 'tripotages tunisiens' denounced by Rochefort may arouse general indignation, but, he assures us, they are simply typical of all diplomatic and political dealings: 'Nous vivons sous le règne du pot-de-vin, dans le royaume de la conscience facile, à genoux devant le veau d'or' ('Choses du jour', *6*, I, p. 373). (Ironically enough, Maupassant himself, the 'industriel des lettres', is caricatured by the venomous Léon Bloy as 'Gilles de Vaudoré' in his novel *Le Désespéré* (1886).)

Occasionally, there is an attempt to take a more positive position: no one can believe in politics,

> ... ces balivernes qu'on nomme relations internationales [...] ce jeu de colin-maillard où s'adonnent ces aveugles-nés, braillards vides, intrigants, craqueurs, bateleurs, farceurs, trompeurs, qu'on appelle les hommes politiques [...]. Une seule opinion, soit dit en passant, me semble raisonnable, celle des anarchistes révolutionnaires. Ceux-là, du moins, quel que soit le gouvernement, sont ses ennemis, en vertu de ce principe que quiconque gouverne abuse des autres, les trompe et les pille.   ('Contemporains', *6*, I, p. 323)

But one is prepared to take revolutionary anarchists seriously only if they occasionally leave their yachts or studies and put in an appearance on the barricades. Writers who were genuine revolutionaries or libertarians in Maupassant's time received harsh treatment from the authorities – after the Paris Commune, Vallès was sentenced to death *in absentia* and spent a decade in exile, while Louise Michel was transported to New Caledonia, along with Henri Rochefort, to name three famous figures. Even Zola earned a prison sentence for his intervention in the Dreyfus Affair in 1898. The trouble with Maupassant is that while he despises the governing classes, doubtless with much justification, at the same time he has no belief in the efficacy of any sort of political action, and no sense of solidarity with the people. Whereas Vallès maintained that all writing was ultimately political, insofar as it either supported or subverted the ideology of the ruling order (and his novel *L'Enfant* (1879) skilfully demonstrates how the dominant cultural modes of the mid-nineteenth century are part of the orthodoxy of oppression), Maupassant explicitly distances himself from this sort of all-embracing conception of politics. Vallès, he observes somewhat maliciously, is rather more successful as a novelist than as a politician; the values of art exceed those of politics ('Va t'asseoir!', 6, I, pp. 277-78). And though Maupassant's books reach a mass audience, particularly in the twentieth century, he himself is an élitist both politically and aesthetically; 'nous ne sommes pas du peuple. L'Art, quel qu'il soit, ne s'adresse qu'à l'aristocratie intellectuelle d'un pays' ('A propos du peuple', 6, II, p. 274).

As Hubert Juin astutely remarks, Maupassant's 'anar-chism' is that of the *petit employé* who distrusts the author-ities above him and despises the masses below him: 'Témoin, Maupassant est insurpassable. Commentateur, il devient faux témoin' (6, I, p. 6). His blithe judgement (noted earlier) that the lot of an *employé* is as bad as or worse than a miner's is a good illustration of a fundamental lack of sympathy for the working classes. Nor is he really a very serious anti-colonialist – he protests against the exploitation of Arabs for purely commercial interests, but in a tell-tale aside on the 'childlike' nature of the Arab reveals that he shares the paternalistic sense of innate superiority of the European coloniser ('Lettre d'Afrique', 6, I, p. 271). Left-wing critics have often complained that Zola refuses to envisage a polit-ical or economic solution to the wretched conditions of the miners in *Germinal*: he constantly shifts from documentary materialism to poeticised mythmaking – Capital is locked away in a distant, impenetrable tabernacle, like some unseen sinister God; at best one can sow the dragon's teeth of future

Revolution. But nevertheless, it is hard to deny the overriding humanitarianism of *Germinal,* the moving sense of solidarity in suffering and possibilities of renewal which unite both characters and also author and reader. *Bel-Ami,* on the contrary, reflects a morality that is entirely egotistical: as successful *parvenu,* Duroy has no class solidarity, any more than he believes in conventional humane values. Maupassant is not really interested in social reform: if society is corrupt, one must learn to play the rules of its absurd game. 'Le monde est aux forts' (II, 2), and all suffering is determined by 'l'impitoyable nature' (II, 4).

One returns, then, to a view of Maupassant as a naturalist, a writer for whom personal and social problems are ultimately determined, not by ideological or political conflict, but by fixed natural forces. This is not to deny that *Bel-Ami* is a novel which presents a historically accurate picture of the Third Republic in the 1880s, and that within its limits Maupassant's unflattering image of politicians is a valid form of criticism. Louis Daquin's film of the novel in 1955 emphasised its anti-colonialist aspects and was promptly banned, finally appearing only in a censored version. To take this as proof that *Bel-Ami* is some sort of revolutionary work, however, is somewhat ingenuous:

> ... ce roman témoin était une telle critique de la société de son temps qu'aujourd'hui encore, sa mise à l'écran fit se lever, lorsque Louis Daquin le porta à l'écran, les barrières imbéciles mais évidentes de la Censure. (*35,* p. 206)

As was observed, this was one way of celebrating the book's seventieth anniversary (its hundredth anniversary in 1985 seems to have passed virtually unnoticed, thanks to 'l'année Victor Hugo'). Another supporter of Daquin (a member of the French Communist Party, like his scriptwriters Roger Vailland and Wladimir Pozner) wrote, again with a degree of disingenuousness:

> En tout état de cause, il reste que les événements racontés à l'écran sont typiquement ceux du temps de Jules Ferry, non

> pas ceux d'aujourd'hui. L'histoire aussi sera-t-elle frappée de
> censure? [...] On le voit clairement: c'est précisément cette
> fidélité à l'Histoire, telle qu'elle fut et non pas telle qu'on
> voudrait la faire enseigner, qui irrite le gouvernement.   (*18*,
> pp. 135, 137)

Such protestations by a hardline communist literary review in
favour of a communist director may have a hollow ring, since
fidelity to history is hardly one of their party's hallmarks.
The most obvious reasons for the censoring of the film seem,
in retrospect, extrinsic to Maupassant's novel: the mid-fifties
marked the beginning of the undeclared but bloody war of
independence in Algeria, with its thousands of casualties,
sickening atrocities on both sides, and bitter legacy of hatred.
In a period which saw the threat of military dictatorship in
France and the eventual collapse of the Fourth Republic as a
result of the crisis, it is hardly surprising that the authorities
were hypersensitive to anything smacking of anti-colonialist
propaganda.

The word naturalism has several different, though over-
lapping, connotations when applied to writing in the late
nineteenth century. Maupassant's relationship with Zola is
sometimes seen as proof of his commercial opportunism: he
published his first major work, 'Boule de Suif', in *Les Soirées
de Médan* (1880), a collection of stories by naturalist writers
who formed a group under Zola, but Maupassant subsequently refused to be presented as a disciple in the naturalist
'school'. Louis Forestier warns that 'Aborder Maupassant par
le biais de son appartenance ou non au naturalisme risque de
créer un faux problème, sans apporter grand éclaircissement
sur l'originalité de l'écrivain' (*7*, I, p. xxx). If naturalism is
seen in a wider sense, however, as a particular set of beliefs
which produces a certain type of writing (which could be
crudely encapsulated in the terms determinism, documenta-
tion and description), it does not seem far-fetched to place
Maupassant both historically and critically as a naturalist. I
have already tried to suggest how his descriptive writing does
more than simply provide a convincing décor for his characters: without its descriptions, *Bel-Ami* would collapse into

fantastic melodrama; the landscape is often more vital and appealing than the figures who move across it. While Zola is famous for promoting the notion of the novel as sociological enquiry – his *Rougon-Macquart* cycle supposedly combines social and natural history – clearly *Bel-Ami* is Maupassant's most ambitious attempt at a social documentary, where fiction combines private drama with a commentary on public events. Again, one can hardly deny that Maupassant is a determinist. The lives of his characters are circumscribed by forces beyond their conscious control. Women, for instance, are usually defined by their social relationships with men (wife, prostitute, spinster) and by their biological function as reproductive vessels (mother, virgin). A story like 'Aux champs' provides a model demonstration of how character can be totally created by social environment: the Vallins' son is sold to a rich childless couple and becomes a gentleman; the Tuvaches turn down the offer and their son remains a yokel. Two destinies are moulded by decisions deliberately presented as arbitrary and reversible.

Robert Lethbridge refers to Maupassant's 'literary Darwinism' in *Bel-Ami,* and reminds us that his determinism is biological as much as social: 'Maupassant's materialist conception of experience is essentially vitalist, in so far as he presents human beings as a species subject to natural laws too' (*50,* p. 33). The obsession with illegitimacy in *Pierre et Jean* and elsewhere is symptomatic of a more far-reaching drama of biological origins; Pierre's happiness is destroyed by the discovery of his mother's fall, even though he himself, of course, is not illegitimate. An anonymous article in *Le Télégraphe* of 14 May 1885 attacked 'Le Darwinisme littéraire' of both Zola and *Bel-Ami*:

> Jamais, jusqu'à présent, le manque de talent, de conscience et de sens moral, jamais la sauvagerie du désir et la brutalité sensuelle de l'amour n'avaient trouvé une plus complaisante apothéose.   (Quoted in *60,* p. 278)

This is not the place to summarise the history of social Darwinism – Linda L. Clark's recent scholarly study of *Social*

Darwinism in France (Alabama, University Press, 1984) does not in any case contain a single reference to Maupassant. What is essentially involved is the application of analogies from the natural world to human society – Duroy as the incarnation of a ferocious predatory energy, a forerunner of Zola's 'bête humaine'. The point one wants to retain is made by Micheline Besnard-Coursodon:

> Maupassant n'est pas un écrivain social; il a trop profondément le sentiment de la misère humaine pour la limiter à son côté social – donc contingent – simple aspect à ses yeux du déterminisme fondamental inhérent à notre condition d'homme.   (*19*, p. 103)

Duroy refuses the determinism of nature by rejecting the biological truths which the novel presents – he escapes death and sickness, or engaging in communication with the other, or even probing his own self – but in doing so becomes the pure creation of social forces where authentic values are turned into the ambiguous spectacle of success. *Bel-Ami* is not a political novel because the domain of politics is not seen as a reality but as a charade cut off from the vital forces which tragically govern the world.

Maupassant and the Novel

I s it in fact reasonable, or meaningful, to ask the reader to *like Bel-Ami?* It is true that lack of sympathy for an author may lead one to underestimate his talents. Maupassant has certainly suffered enough from this in the past. In 1941, Artine Artinian published an 'Inquiry into the present fame of Maupassant' as an appendix to his *Maupassant Criticism in France (14)*; this was subsequently expanded in 1955 to *Pour et contre Maupassant (15)*, which consists of 147 'témoignages' from well-known writers and critics, as many of whom prove to be dismissive as sympathetic. However interesting such brief evaluative contributions may be, they hardly amount to serious criticism. Unlike some modern writers and artists whose reputation seems largely to have been fabricated by a handful of intellectuals and critics, Maupassant has always spoken directly to his public. *Bel-Ami* had reached its thirty-seventh printing within three months of publication, and its fifty-first within two years, a good sale for the time, though not spectacularly so (Zola's relatively little known novel *L'Argent* sold 50,000 copies within a few days of its appearance in 1891, for example). Maupassant does not need criticism to promote his cause, in this sense. One suspects that the invariably sour comments which Edmond de Goncourt makes about him in his *Journal* (Maupassant has the aesthetic sensibility of a West Indian pimp, he avers) are inspired by envy of such undeserved commercial popularity. In any case, criticism has subsequently caught up with public esteem: Maupassant's stories and novels have been enshrined in Gallimard's prestigious Pléiade collection, and the second volume of stories was promoted by the somewhat comic spectacle of President Giscard d'Estaing debating the author's

genius on a TV book programme with the university professor responsible for the edition.

Criticism rarely, if ever, succeeds in pinning down the
secret of Maupassant's popular appeal, if indeed it bothers to
attempt to do so. Yet if the reader likes *Bel-Ami,* it is probably
in the first instance precisely because it makes for entertain-
ing reading. We are engaged with a character who has a
strong physical presence, who moves in an easily identifiable
social world, and whose actions are presented in a conventional linear narrative. Alain Robbe-Grillet states bluntly, in
a revealing aside in *Pour un nouveau roman,* that 'raconter
pour distraire est futile'. Certainly no one could accuse
Robbe-Grillet of this. Such highbrow priggishness blithely
ignores the reasons for which most people read books – to be
informed and entertained. Few people would deny that *No
Orchids for Miss Blandish* provokes a much stronger emotional response and is much more compelling reading than
Le Voyeur, even if both James Hadley Chase and Robbe-
Grillet offer us portraits of psychopathic murderers. But such
readability ultimately excludes any concept of literary value;
one does not have to be an intellectual puritan to know that
facility carried beyond a certain point produces trashy formula-writing. There is also little doubt that Maupassant at his
worst comes dangerously close to this sort of facility – a neat
anecdote held in a convenient framework, presenting a glib,
cynical illustration of human pretensions and frailty, enliv-
ened if possible with a touch of carefully measured bawdy
humour or a few lyrical evocations of nature, the great
equaliser.

Reading *Bel-Ami* does not create either the intellectual or
formal demands which the reader is likely to experience
when confronted with Balzac, Stendhal, Flaubert or Proust.
Maupassant has little of their density or impenetrability. On
the simplest level, the financial jiggery-pokery of *Bel-Ami*
seems mere childsplay compared with the machinations of
M. Grandet in *Eugénie Grandet* (1833): the reader of Balzac
has to fight through a jungle of miscellaneous information
which overgrows the path of a unilinear story. Both Flaubert
and Proust teasingly offer the reader a sense of story, and then

withdraw it: our desire for a straightforward sequence of events and actions is frustrated and subverted. While Bel-Ami fulfils all his goals in a way that is satisfying yet also monotonous, Emma Bovary is denied such simple fulfilment (she waits eternally to be invited again to the ball at La Vaubyessard) and in Proust an event like a train ride can be prolonged over dozens or hundreds of pages, so that it becomes pointless to look for plot in the conventional sense. Again, Maupassant's carefully constructed narrative, with its neat set of episodes and sympathetic but unobtrusive narrator, is remote from the mannered tone of carefree ellipsis which is likely to bemuse and infuriate the reader coming to grips with Stendhal for the first time.

Is there any need to apologise for spelling out the weaknesses of *Bel-Ami,* or is it not merely sensible to do so if one wants to judge Maupassant's contribution to French fiction? The central complaint might be that he makes things too easy, for Duroy, for himself, and for the reader. Just as Duroy exploits conventional social morality for his success, so too Maupassant produces a novel which, whatever its air of social criticism, is highly conventional in technique and promotes his own career as writer perfectly happy to accept the accolades of a society he affects to despise. As we have seen, Maupassant had little interest in the condition of the industrial working class, and was incapable of producing novels like Zola's *L'Assommoir* (1877) and *Germinal.* While the workers appear only briefly as exotic fauna in *Bel-Ami* when Mme de Marelle satisfies her urge for low-life by visiting sleazy cafés with Duroy (I, 5) (though she is outraged when a lower-class woman insults her on the stairs of his tenement), Zola achieved a radical extension in both the form and content of the French novel in a work like *L'Assommoir,* not simply by making urban workers his central characters – though this was radical enough – but also by allowing their thought processes and speech habits to take over the language of the text, so that the reader is brutally confronted from the inside with a world he knows little about. However equivocal Zola's own political attitudes may have been, his ambition to give the bourgeois reader 'un frisson de terreur' when present-

ed with *Germinal* suggests that he wanted his fiction to have
an impact that combined the emotional and the ideological.

While Maupassant's first novel, *Une Vie* (1883), clearly
looks back twenty-six years to *Madame Bovary,* his contemporary Huysmans began by producing studies of urban life
like *Les Sœurs Vatard* (1879) which try to follow Zola's
innovatory manner. However, Huysmans' masterpiece, *A
rebours* (1884), overturns the conventions of the documentary novel of social manners which Maupassant obeys in
Bel-Ami. While Duroy slavishly and skilfully apes the behav-
ioural norms of the particular social group he arrives in, and
the plot of *Bel-Ami* is essentially built around a series of
social tableaux which clearly create a sense of linear progression in terms of narrative (even if we may doubt that there is
any real progress in absolute terms), Huysmans' hero des
Esseintes, on the other hand, attempts to reject all social
and biological norms by retreating into complete isolation,
and the plot of *A rebours* recounts the fantasies, memories and
reflexions which pass through his mind as he remains fixed
inside his 'refined Thebaid' at Fontenay-aux-Roses. Nevertheless both Huysmans and Maupassant share a rather
similar cynical view of social mechanisms. Des Esseintes is
famous as a model of 'decadence', but in fact his solipsistic
project is an attempt to redefine his own identity and cultural
norms in the face of a society whose values are adulterated
and decadent. And in the case of *Bel-Ami,* Sartre has observed that the degree of Duroy's success merely shows him
to be a sort of thermometer all too accurately gauging the
decadence of his society.

Maupassant's later novels, which tend from *Pierre et
Jean* onwards to portray isolated heroes confronting personal dramas, come closer to Huysmans' solipsistic plot in *A
rebours,* where the action is a function of one character's
thought processes. But unlike Huysmans, Maupassant never
rejects the framework of the story which recounts a clearly
defined sequence of events in a specific social setting. Nor
does he reject the descriptive baggage and neutral narrative
perspective of the naturalist novel. He never permits himself
the personal, playful tone one finds in writers like Jules

Vallès or Georges Darien, with their outrageous puns, self-deprecating heroes and loose-jointed narrative structure. By suggesting that conventional fictional forms are part of a wider cultural and ideological system of repression, such authors produce novels which are far more radical than Maupassant's, and far more authentic as social criticism.

Yet however convinced one may be that *A rebours, L'Enfant* and *Le Voleur* are much more interesting and probably better novels than *Bel-Ami,* it is an undoubted fact that even if one gets the chance to harangue a captive audience in professorial fashion, experience soon shows that most of its members will invariably read *Bel-Ami,* if they read anything at all. Is it simply because Maupassant is a good, undemanding read, with the added advantage of being consecrated by literary history, the cinema, and television, while even so-called specialists in the French novel rarely bother to open a work by Darien, whose place in the reference books is far from assured? I do not think it is a service to Maupassant to invest his work with a profundity or intellectual complexity which it does not really possess. In *Bel-Ami,* he has created a hero who is memorable for the way in which he converts his initial vulnerability into the appearance of social and sexual mastery. While Julien Sorel in *Le Rouge et le Noir* finally rejects the pretence of social existence, returning to the core of essential naturalness which we are expected to believe he always possesses, however disreputable his behaviour, and Stendhal thus casts him as a typical heroic Romantic outcast, one could argue that Maupassant's portrayal of Duroy shows a more modern, existentialist view of the self: Duroy has no essential inner being but is almost entirely defined by his acts, by the images which others and the world reflect back at him. *Bel-Ami* is a successful novel not because it presents a richly complex protagonist moving in a massively detailed and historically accurate social setting, but because Maupassant has suggested the ambiguous, compromised position of the individual engaged with society. It is no longer enough to go nobly to the gallows, or sit on a rock in the desert contemplating eternity; we are caught up and corrupted by the social process, and yet its ephemeral rewards are all we can set against universal annihilation, to which the weak submit all too readily.

Above all, however, Maupassant should be remembered as a storyteller. At his best he can take an anecdote that seems sordid or trite and invest it with an immediacy, an emotional resonance which conveys poignant and simple truths about human emotions and failings with deliberate understatement. Gérard Delaisement has pointed out that Maupassant plundered as many as thirty of his stories and fifty of his articles in the composition of *Bel-Ami*. In some cases, episodes in the novel may have been used subsequently in stories, rather than the reverse, but Delaisement notes that there is only one undisputed example of this, the story 'Le Legs', a close transposition of the chapter dealing with Vaudrec's legacy (II, 6), published in *Gil Blas* on 23 September 1884, and significantly never republished in any of the collections which appeared during Maupassant's lifetime. But as this critic observes, 'Au fur et à mesure qu'analogies et ressemblances se multiplient, elles perdent de leur importance matérielle' (*28*, p. 226). What is clearer, if one contrasts the longer and shorter pieces of fiction, is that Maupassant does not need the vehicle of a 400-page novel to achieve his greatest effects. Perhaps he really did lack the fundamental intelligence and imaginative range to produce a novel equal to the subtle intricacy of *L'Education sentimentale*; but it is the very brevity and crisp immediacy of a masterpiece like 'Boule de Suif' which engages the reader's emotions in a way far more effective than the overwritten and overdetermined pieces which make up Flaubert's *Trois contes,* which in comparison seem like problematic *exercices de style.* Although in the final analysis *Bel-Ami* seems somewhat unadventurous in its use of conventional fictional forms, we should not forget that Maupassant's success in capturing the reader's interest and endowing the adventures of his *arriviste* with an exemplary status is due to an artistry which is all the more admirable for its unobtrusive modesty.

Bibliography

T H E reader seeking further information on *Bel-Ami* should in the first instance consult critical editions of the novel: the best is that edited by Marie-Claire Bancquart (item *4* below). By far the most interesting and informative introduction to Maupassant's life and work is the edition of his correspondence in three volumes edited by J. Suffel (*11*); unfortunately this edition is not easy to get hold of. The biographical studies by Armand Lanoux (*48*) and Francis Steegmuller (*54*) are readable and thorough. Edward D. Sullivan (*55*) and André Vial (*60*) have written the most useful critical accounts of Maupassant's craft as a novelist for the non-specialised reader.

WORKS BY MAUPASSANT

1. *Bel-Ami*, ed. Gérard Delaisement (Garnier, 1959)
2. *Bel-Ami*, preface and notes by Jean-Louis Bory (Gallimard, Folio, 1973)
3. *Bel-Ami*, translation and introduction by Douglas Parmée (Harmondsworth, Penguin, 1975)
4. *Bel-Ami*, ed. Marie-Claire Bancquart (Imprimerie nationale, 1979)
5. *Bel-Ami*, preface by Jacques Laurent, commentary and notes by Philippe Bonnefis (Le Livre de Poche, 1983)
6. *Chroniques*, preface by Hubert Juin, 3 vols (Union Générale d'Editions, 10/18, 1980)
7. *Contes et nouvelles*, ed. Louis Forestier, 2 vols (Gallimard, Pléiade, 1974 and 1979)
8. *Etudes, chroniques et correspondance*, ed. René Dumesnil, vol. 15 of *Œuvres complètes illustrées* (Librairie de France, 1938)
9. *Maupassant journaliste et chroniqueur*, ed. Gérard Delaisement (Albin Michel, 1956)
10. *Œuvres complètes*, 29 unnumbered vols (Conard, 1908-10)
11. *Œuvres complètes: correspondance*, ed. J. Suffel, 3 vols (Geneva, Edito-Service, 1973)
12. *Romans*, ed. Albert-Marie Schmidt (Albin Michel, 1975)
12a. *Romans*, ed. Louis Forestier (Gallimard, Pléiade, 1987)

OTHER SOURCES CONSULTED

13. Andry, Marc, *Bel-Ami, c'est moi!* (Presses de la Cité, 1983)
14. Artinian, Artine, *Maupassant Criticism in France 1880-1940* (New York, King's Crown Press, 1941)

15. Artinian, Artine, *Pour et contre Maupassant* (Nizet, 1955)

16. Artinian, Robert Willard, and Artinian, Artine, *Maupassant Criticism: a centennial bibliography 1880-1979* (Jefferson and London, McFarland, 1982)

17. Bancquart, Marie-Claire, 'Maupassant et l'argent', *Romantisme,* 40 (1983), 129-39

18. Bernardin, François, 'Le Scandale de *Bel-Ami*', *La Nouvelle Critique,* 7 (May 1955), 126-38

19. Besnard-Coursodon, Micheline, *Etude thématique et structurale de l'œuvre de Maupassant: le piège* (Nizet, 1973)

20. Bismut, Roger, 'Quelques problèmes de création littéraire dans *Bel-Ami*', *Revue d'histoire littéraire de la France,* 67 (1967), 577-89

21. Borie, Jean, *Le Célibataire français* (Sagittaire, 1976)

22. Brunetière, Ferdinand, 'Le Pessimisme dans le roman', *Revue des deux mondes* (1 July 1885), 214-26

23. Castella, Charles, *Structures romanesques et vision sociale chez Maupassant* (Lausanne, L'Age d'Homme, 1972)

24. Chaikin, Milton, 'Maupassant's *Bel-Ami* and Balzac', *Romance Notes,* 1 (1960), 109-12

25. Daquin, Louis, 'Le Film *Bel-Ami* et la censure', *Le Bel-Ami* (1961), 11-16

26. Dard, Frédéric, '*Bel-Ami.* Pièce en 2 actes et 8 tableaux d'après l'œuvre de Guy de Maupassant', *Paris-Théâtre,* 82 (March 1954), 21-55

27. Delaisement, Gérard, 'L'Univers de *Bel-Ami*', *Revue des sciences humaines,* 69 (January-March 1953), 77-87

28. ———, '*Bel-Ami* et les écrits antérieurs de Maupassant', *Revue des sciences humaines,* 82 (April-June 1956), 195-228

29. ———, 'La Composition des *Carnets de voyages* de Guy de Maupassant', *Revue des sciences humaines,* 92 (October-December 1958), 531-54

30. ———, 'La Publication de *Bel-Ami* et l'affaire Deschaumes', *Le Bel-Ami* (1961), 19-21

31. ———, *Bel-Ami* (Hatier, Profil d'une œuvre, 1972)

32. Dugan, John Raymond, *Illusion and Reality: a study of descriptive techniques in the works of Guy de Maupassant* (The Hague, Mouton, 1973)

33. Dumesnil, René, *Guy de Maupassant* (Armand Colin, 1933)

34. Dupuy, Aimé, '*Bel-Ami* et les origines du protectorat français en Tunisie', *Le Monde* (19 February 1955)

35. *Europe,* 482, issue on 'Guy de Maupassant' (June 1969)

36. *La femme au XIXe siècle* (Lyon, Presses Universitaires de Lyon, 1979)

37. *Flaubert et Maupassant écrivains normands* (Presses Universitaires de France, 1981)

38. Grant, Richard B., 'The Function of the First Chapter of Maupassant's *Bel-Ami*', *Modern Language Notes,* 76 (1961), 748-52

39. Greimas, Algirdas Julien, *Maupassant: la sémiotique du texte. Exercices pratiques* (Seuil, 1976)

40. Hainsworth, G., 'Pattern and Symbol in the Work of Maupassant', *French Studies,* 5 (1951), 1-17

41. Hamilton, James F., 'The Impossible Return to Nature in Maupassant's *Bel-Ami*: or the intellectual heroine as deviant', *Nineteenth-Century French Studies,* 10 (1982), 326-39

42. *Histoire générale de la presse française,* ed. Claude Bellanger et al., vol. 3, *1871-1940* (Presses Universitaires de France, 1972)

43. Ignotus, Paul, *The Paradox of Maupassant* (London, University Press, 1966)

44. Jacob, Pierre, '*Bel-Ami*: le film, le roman et l'histoire', *La Nouvelle Critique,* 7 (February 1955), 141-46

45. Jennings, Chantal, 'La Dualité de Maupassant: son attitude envers la femme', *Revue des sciences humaines,* 140 (October-December 1970), 559-78

46. Lajeune-Vilar, André, *Les Coulisses de la presse: mœurs et chantages du journalisme* (Charles, 1895)

47. Lanoux, Armand, '*Bel-Ami* octogénaire ou le roman d'un roman', *A la page* (September 1965), 1298-1307

48. ———, *Maupassant le Bel-Ami* (Fayard, 1967; reprinted Le Livre de Poche, 1979)

49. Lerner, Michael G., *Maupassant* (London, Allen and Unwin, 1975)

50. Lethbridge, Robert, *Maupassant: 'Pierre et Jean'* (London, Grant and Cutler, 1984)

51. Nicholas, B. L., 'Maupassant', in *French Literature and its Background: the late nineteenth century,* ed. John Cruickshank (London, Oxford University Press, 1969), 116-31

52. Nørreslet, Eva, 'Analyse de *Bel-Ami*', *Revue romane,* 6 (1971), 233-42

53. Schmidt, Albert-Marie, *Maupassant par lui-même* (Seuil, 1962)

54. Steegmuller, Francis, *Maupassant* (London, Collins, 1950)

55. Sullivan, Edward D., *Maupassant the Novelist* (New Jersey, Princeton University Press, 1954; reprinted Westport, Greenwood Press, 1978)

56. Tassart, François, *Souvenirs sur Guy de Maupassant* (Plon, 1911)

57. ———, *Nouveaux Souvenirs intimes sur Guy de Maupassant,* ed. Pierre Cogny (Nizet, 1962)

58. Thibaudet, Albert, 'La Question *Bel-Ami*', in *Réflexions sur la littérature,* vol. 2 (Gallimard, 1941), 223-28

59. Vial, André, '*Bel-Ami*: roman de la conquête de la Tunisie', *Les Lettres françaises* (8 July 1954)

60. ———, *Guy de Maupassant et l'art du roman* (Nizet, 1954)

61. Weisstein, Ulrich, 'Maupassant's *Bel-Ami* and Heinrich Mann's *Im Schlaraffenland*', *Romance Notes,* 2, (1961), 124-28

CRITICAL GUIDES TO FRENCH TEXTS

edited by
Roger Little, Wolfgang van Emden, David Williams